Lady Aud...

o...

Death in Lime Tree Walk

BY THE SAME AUTHOR:—

THE HOUSE OF ROSMER
(Adapted from Ibsen)

THE MURDER OF MARIA MARTEN
or
THE RED BARN
(Based on various Victorian texts)

EAST LYNNE
or
LADY ISABEL'S SHAME
(Based on the novel by Mrs. Henry Wood)

SWEENEY TODD THE BARBER
(Adapted from G. D. Pitt)

THE DRUNKARD
or
DOWN WITH DEMON DRINK
(Based on the version by W. H. Smith)

THREE HISSES FOR VILLAINY ! ! !
(Three one-act melodramas)

THE WOODPILE
(A modern three-act drama)

LINES OF COMMUNICATION
(Eight short plays for two players)

Lady Audley's Secret

or

Death in Lime Tree Walk

a melodrama in three acts by

BRIAN J. BURTON

based on various Victorian dramatisations and the novel by Mary Braddon

HANBURY PLAYS
KEEPER'S LODGE
BROUGHTON GREEN
DROITWICH
WORCESTERSHIRE WR9 7EE

© Brian J. Burton 1966
1974 1981

This play is fully protected by copyright and is subject to a royalty. All enquiries concerning the rights for amateur stage performance or public reading should be addressed to the publishers:

COMBRIDGE [JACKSON] ... uiries concerning professional [...] made to HUGHES MASSIE LTD., [...] ondon, WC1B 5HL.

FOR PERFORMING RIGHTS APPLY:-
SAMUEL FRENCH LTD.
52 FITZROY STREET
LONDON W1P 6JR

THIS PLAY MAY NOT BE PERFORMED UNLESS
PRIOR PERMISSION HAS BEEN GIVEN

Enquiries concerning performances or public readings should be made to the following:

UNITED STATES OF AMERICA:- Samuel French Inc., 24 West 45th Street, New York, NY 10056.
CANADA:- Samuel French (Canada) Ltd., 80 Richmond Street, East Toronto, M5C 1P1.
AUSTRALIA:- Samuel French (Aust.) Pty. Ltd., 8 Cross Street, Brookvale, Sydney, NSW.
NEW ZEALAND:- Play Bureau (N.Z.) Ltd., P.O. Box 3611, Wellington.

Printed by Leslie G. Hill, Worcester

INTRODUCTION

Mary Elizabeth Braddon (1837-1915) made her reputation as a writer with her novel 'Lady Audley's Secret' which she wrote when she was still in her early twenties. First published in 'The Sixpenny Magazine', it was issued as a separate work in 1862. She wrote many more novels and some plays and, for a time, was editor of several magazines including 'Belgravia' and 'Temple Bar'. She was also a contributor to 'Punch'.

The first dramatisation of 'Lady Audley's Secret' was by William E. Suter. This was first presented at the Queens Theatre in Tottenham Court Road on February 21st, 1863. Although described as 'a drama in two acts' it is, in fact, a strange mixture of melodrama and naive comedy. The cast includes a butler and footman called Bibbles and Bubbles and much of the play is devoted to their cross-talk act. This was published by Lacy.

Exactly a week after the opening of the Suter version, the best of the three Victorian adaptations opened at the Theatre Royal, St. James with the manageress, Louisa Herbert in the title role. It was an immediate success. Although it was no longer than the other versions – little more than an hour's playing time – it was reasonably faithful to the novel and much nearer in style to the plays of the later Victorian period of Pinero and Robertson than the melodramas of the time. It was, of course, written as a serious social drama although it would be impossible to present it as such today. Nevertheless, Roberts's method of condensing a long Victorian novel into an hour's play was admirable and I have used his adaptation as a framework for my dramatisation. This version was not published but is to be found in the collection of manuscripts from the Lord Chamberlain's Office lodged at the British Museum.

The best known version – that of C. H. Hazlewood – was first presented at the Royal Victoria Theatre (later to become the home of the 'Old Vic.') on May 25th, 1863. Hazlewood was a prolific writer and was responsible for over a hundred plays and dramatisations of novels. For many years he was resident dramatist at the Britannia Theatre in Hoxton. His version is in the old style of melodrama and, in fact, does not include one line of Mary Braddon's novel and he forgets completely to tell his audience what Lady Audley's secret was. The text was published in 1864 and is available today in a volume of collected Victorian drama.

I would like to express my gratitude to the staff of the British Museum for valuable assistance with original manuscripts and to Laurence Neal and the Leicester Little Theatre Company for their excellent production of my new version of the play.

BRIAN J. BURTON.
1966

To my daughter
ELIZABETH

CHARACTERS IN THE PLAY

ROBERT AUDLEY—*a barrister-at-law*
GEORGE TALBOYS—*his friend*
LUKE MARKS—*a gamekeeper*
PHOEBE MARKS—*his cousin, a lady's maid*
LADY AUDLEY—*married to Sir Michael*
ALICIA AUDLEY—*her step-daughter*
SIR MICHAEL AUDLEY—*a gentleman*
MARTIN—*a parlourmaid*

SYNOPSIS OF SCENES

ACT ONE:	*Scene One:*	Robert Audley's chambers in Fig Tree Court, Temple. A summer's morning in the 1850's
	Scene Two:	Lime Tree Walk in the grounds of Audley Court a few weeks later
	Scene Three:	The Library at Audley Court – later the same day
	Scene Four:	Lime Tree Walk – dusk the same evening
ACT TWO:	*Scene One:*	The Library – twelve months later
	Scene Two:	Lime Tree Walk – fifteen minutes later
	Scene Three:	The Castle Inn at Mount Stanning – later that night
ACT THREE:	*Scene One:*	Lime Tree Walk – later that night
	Scene Two:	The Library – the next day
	Scene Three:	Lime Tree Walk – a few minutes later

LADY AUDLEY'S SECRET or DEATH IN LIME TREE WALK was first presented at the Little Theatre, Leicester on 9th, February 1966, with the following cast:—

ROBERT AUDLEY....................Ian Rodger
GEORGE TALBOYS..................Peter Adams
LUKE MARKS.....................John Saunders
PHOEBE MARKS.................Barbara Kenney
LADY AUDLEY...................Darien Thomas
ALICIA AUDLEY.................Sylvia Deveson
SIR MICHAEL AUDLEY............Brian Daubney
MARTIN........................Pamela Rodger

The play was directed by LAURENCE NEAL
with settings designed by ROY SMITH
Photographs by GEORGE KELMAN

ACT ONE
SCENE ONE

Music before curtain (cue 1).
Robert Audley's chambers in Fig Tree Court, Temple. A summer's morning in the 1850's.

There is a table left centre with a chair upstage of it and another to the left of it. There is a sofa right centre.

(Note: Throughout the play, only the furniture referred to in the stage directions is mentioned in the description of the settings).

When the curtain rises, ROBERT AUDLEY, *a handsome, lazy, care-for-nothing fellow of 27, is seated upstage of the table reading the Times.*

Robert: Copper moping, pig-iron dull. Nothing very exciting today. I think I'll read this letter before I settle down to read the rest of Sir Oracle. *(Puts down the paper and picks up a letter from the table)* Robert Audley Esq., Barrister-at Law. This is my pretty cousin's handywork, I'll be bound. That's Alicia's idea of a joke – a note of admiration at one end and a note of interrogation at the other. She's never content unless she's pitching into me. For five years I've listened to the advice of friends and foes. 'Go to Westminster' says one 'and ventilate yourself'. So I would if they'd ventilate the courts. 'Stick to Chambers and wait for clients' whispers a second'. 'Go circuit' bellows a third. Circuit – phew! Haven't I been round and round and round again like a squirrel in a cage, till I've lapsed into a state of chronic vertigo? Still, what with a trip up the Rhine or a peep at the Pyrenees, a day's cover shooting to say nothing of a stall at the opera and a cozy club, I manage to scratch through the year somehow. Then there's my Uncle's honest face and his ever cheery welcome at Audley Court and Alicia; Alicia! That reminds me of her letter. *(He opens the letter)* Crossed and recrossed of course, and stuffed with the usual padding, abuse of Sir Michael's young bride and mild banter about my legal deficiencies– oh, what's this? 'Papa expects you to come as soon as business will permit, and pay your homage to the wax doll'. Wax doll? That must be Alicia's description of my new aunt. 'She is

dying to make your acquaintance'. Poor Alicia! There is clearly not room for two rival queens at Audley Court. Dying to make my acquaintance, is she? Well, I'll gratify her. I'll go, for I'm anxious I own it, to see this raven-haired Circe who has taken captive sober sixty-five. Yes, my servant shall pack my bag at once and I'll run down there this very afternoon.
  (*A knocking up right*).
Robert: A knock! (*rising and moving up right*). It is too soft for a dun and too loud for a lady. I wonder who it can be. (*Exit up right*) Hello! What is it?
George (*off*): Is this Mr. Audley's?
Robert (*off*): Yes, this is Mr. Audley's, my good man – and your business?
George: I'll tell you when I'm inside.
Robert: But I don't know if –
George (*as he enters*): But I do.
Robert (*following* GEORGE *who moves to centre stage*): I've seen you before, my bearded friend but I'll be hanged if I can recall when or where.

   GEORGE TALBOYS *is a tall, powerfully built young man in his late twenties. He is very tanned and has a dark beard.*

George: Do you mean to stand there and tell me you have forgotten your old Eton fag and friend, George Talboys?
Robert (*with unusual emphasis*): George – George Talboys!
  They shake hands.
George: Aye, Bob, the same – though a little worse for wear. I only touched British ground after dark last night. I came up by the morning express and as I was passing through town I thought I must spare a few minutes to call and see my old friend before – before I ran off – to *her* –
Robert: Her?
George: Yes, my wife. But I forgot you don't know the history of my last three years.
Robert: Why, man, how should I? I've neither heard of you nor seen you for many a long day. But just fancy – the idea of you having a wife. Come, sit down and tell me the truth, the whole truth and nothing but the truth.

They sit on the sofa – GEORGE *on the right side.*

George: My story is soon told, Bob. Thanks to the purchase system and my father's assistance, I didn't rest a subaltern long. The monotonous routine of a cavalry regiment didn't bore me too much and despite the inactivity I contrived to exist if not live. At length we were moved to a rotten worm-eaten seaport, so dull and melancholy that, to prevent falling into mischief –

Robert: You fell in love. Much the same thing.

George: Yes, Robert, I did. My pet lived with her father, a broken-down half-pay lieutenant – a drunken old hypocrite ready to sell my poor little girl to the highest bidder. Do you think I didn't see through his shabby-genteel dinners, his public house port, his shallow tricks and contemptible traps?

Robert: Into which you fell nevertheless.

George: I did, but with my eyes wide open. It was love at first sight and we made a match of it. No sooner, however, did my governor hear that I had married a penniless little girl than he wrote me a furious letter, telling me that he would never again hold any communication with me, and that my yearly allowance would stop from my wedding day.

Robert: And so you sold out, of course?

George: Of course. There was no remaining in such a regiment as mine with nothing but my pay to live on and a pretty little wife to keep. I took my darling to Italy and there we lived in splendid style as long as my two thousand pounds lasted. But when that began to dwindle to a couple of hundred or so, we came back to England and as my wife had a fancy for being near that tiresome old father of hers we settled at the watering place where he lived. Drunkard that he was, he proved his affection by draining the dregs of our little stock of money in no time.

Robert: Poor George!

George: However, I had no fear of the future, believing that influence would obtain for me a lucrative appointment.

Robert: And did it not?

George: I went up to London but I could obtain nothing. At

last, tired out and downhearted, I returned to my wife to find her nursing a son and heir to his father's property. When I told her I had failed in everything, she burst into a storm of lamentations. She told me that I ought not to have married her if I could give her nothing but poverty and misery and that I had done her a cruel wrong in making her my wife.
Robert *(surprised)*: She told you that?
George *(rising and moving down right)*: By heavens, Robert, her tears and reproaches drove me almost mad and I rushed from the house, declaring that I would never enter it again.
Robert: And you kept your promise?

Music cue 2.

George *(turning up to* ROBERT*)*: No. The same evening I stole back when she was asleep. She was lying there peacefully sleeping with the baby in her arms. I sat down and wrote a few brief lines which told her that I had never loved her better than now and that I was going to try my fortune in a new world. I told her that if I succeeded I should come back to bring her plenty and happiness but that if I failed I should never look upon her face again. I divided the remainder of our money into two equal portions leaving one for her. Then I kissed her once and the baby once and crept out of the room. Three nights later I was out at sea, bound for Melbourne – a steerage passenger, with a digger's tools for my baggage and about seven shillings in my pocket.

Music ends.

Robert: And you succeeded?
George *(crossing to centre)*: Not until poverty and I had become such old companions that, looking back at my old life, I wondered whether that reckless extravagant dragoon could really be the man who now lay awake under the open sky in the wilds of the new world. *(Turning to face* ROBERT*)* But I clung to the memory of my darling and the trust that I had in her love and truth.
Robert: And then?
George: Then, at last, one dreary foggy morning, a monster nugget turned up under my spade and I came upon a gold

deposit of some magnitude. A month later I was the richest man in the little colony about me.
Robert: But in all that time did you never write to your wife?
George: Never till my luck turned. I could not write when all seemed so black. Then, a week before the vessel set sail, I wrote telling her I should be in England almost as soon as my letter and giving her an address where she could write to me. *(Music cue 3).* I am on my way there now to pick up the letter. *(Music ends).*
Robert: And did you not hear from her while you were in Australia?
George: Not a line – not a word, for three long years or more. But why – how could I when she had no idea of my address? Why do you look so grave?
Robert: Grave? Was I? That's not a common call with me. I was only thinking – never mind.
George: Heavens, man, I read doubt, suspicion in your face. Why do you torture me, when I am going home to the woman I love? To her whose heart is as fixed as the light above, and in whom I no more expect to find a change than I do to see a second sun rise in tomorrow's sky. Why put idle fancies into my head when I am going to her?
Robert *(rising and moving to* GEORGE*)*: My dear George, you are excited and, in the circumstances, I'm not surprised you should be.
George: The *Argus* only got into port late last night. I couldn't wait to see my baggage pass through the customs but came up at once and in a minute I shall be off again for news of my darling wife and before many hours I shall be with her again.
Robert: I only wish I could be with you to share the pleasure of the meeting, George.
George: You shall see her before many days, Bob. *(Sitting on edge of table)* I've made all sorts of plans during the voyage. I shall take a villa on the Thames, Bob, for the little wife and myself, and we'll have a yacht, old fellow, and you shall lie on the deck and smoke while my pretty one plays her guitar and

sings to us, and you shall read your french novels – but I suppose you've done with that style of literature now?
Robert *(sitting on the left end of sofa)*: Not a bit of it.
George: But doesn't it interfere with your practice, Bob?
Robert *(laughing)*: Practice! I didn't give you credit for being such a wag, George.
George: Why, have you given up the Bar?
Robert: Not I. It never gave me the chance – it gave *me* up long ago.
George: Well, you've no cause to complain. You're not poor and you have a rich uncle.
Robert: And as good as he is generous, with as kind a heart as ever beat. But we're none of us fireproof, George, and Cupid's torch has set old Sir Michael alight like so much tinder.
George *(rising and moving to left of* ROBERT*)*: What, married again?
Robert: Yes, George. Half Essex is raving about the new mistress of Audley Court who has bound my uncle by silken chains and raven locks.
George: And how does she agree with you?
Robert: We've never met yet. I thought of running down there this very afternoon.
George: But you've another attraction at Audley Court, if I remember right, Master Bob. There's a certain cousin, isn't there?
Robert: Certain? Uncertain, you mean. George, in my dream hours I've built my castles and villas on the Thames – villas begot and ended in smoke *(rising and moving down right centre)*.
George: Come, come, don't despair; you're destined for something better than drifting away in musty chambers. Not that you're anything but snug and comfortable here.
Robert *(turning to* GEORGE*)*: Yes, I'm comfortable – that's it.
George: But you'd be a great deal more comfortable, if that certain uncertain little party would condescend to take you in hand. She'd effect a wonderful transformation.

Robert: You mean revolution! What would become of the pipes and the cigars?
George: The boxing gloves?
Robert: And Balzac and Dumas and son. There'd be a regular clearance.
George: Under entirely new management, eh, Bob? You'd get business, I know you would – married men always do.
Robert *(sitting on right end of sofa)*: I can't help thinking that if I could find an attorney bold enough to trust me with a brief, I'd do my best.
George *(sitting beside* ROBERT*)*: Best? You'd make a hit, take my word for it.
Robert: That would depend upon the subject. I have a twist for a nice case with all sorts of contradictory clauses or – better still – a good murder. A murder that would do a fellow credit – a tortuous plot, clogged with subtle points of evidence and encumberant with mystery – a case that would take months to master. Gad, George, give me that chance and my reputation's made.
George: I'm afraid I can't get up a murder for you, but I think I'd go as far as a trespass or a breach of the peace to serve an old friend.
Robert *(laughing)*: Thank you – I'll take the will for the deed *(rising and going to table)*. *(Picking up* The Times *and throwing it)* Here, catch! I suppose you haven't seen *The Times* for many a day.
George *(opening the paper and starting to read)* No, a paper from the old country is a rare treat.
Robert *(crossing to left of* GEORGE*)*: Well, George, it's wonderful to see you again and – *(Music cue 4 to end of scene)*. *(Stopping as he sees* GEORGE *staring in horror at the paper)* Heavens, man, what is the matter?
George *(thrusting the paper at* ROBERT*)*: Look, there – there! Under the deaths.
Robert *(reading)*: On the 20th inst. at Ventnor, Isle of Wight, Helen Talboys, aged 21.
George: Helen, my Helen, my wife, my darling, my only love

— dead! Dead! *(Rising and moving away right)*.
Robert: There may have been some other Helen Talboys.
George: No, no, my wife is dead!
Robert *(moving to left of* GEORGE*)*: My poor fellow, what can I say to comfort you?
George: Nothing – nothing. I must bear the sorrow as best I may *(moving up right)*.
Robert: Whither are you going, George?
George: Out into the air – here I am stifled, stifled!
Robert: You will return presently?
George: Yes, yes, have no fear for me. I shall not lay hands on my life. I would pray to Heaven not to outrage it. Oh, Helen! Oh my wife! Dead! Dead!

(Rushes off right).

CURTAIN

Music cue 5.

ACT ONE
SCENE TWO

Music cue 6.

The Lime Tree Walk in the grounds of Audley Court in the County of Essex a few weeks later. This is a front stage scene. There is a garden seat left centre and a crumbling brick well stage right. When the curtain rises LUKE MARKS, *a big stupid-looking clodhopper of 23 is on the seat whittling a piece of wood.*

Luke: Under-keeper at Audley Court! Ugh! You ain't got much of a life, Luke Marks. Under-keeper! I hates being under anybody. I'd like to be independent. If it wasn't for the pickings to be got out of the old Squire's preserves, I'd have been off long ago. *(Chuckling)* A net in the meadow and a wire in the wood, a spring in the spinney and a line in the pond – that's what I call having your own preserves. Well, what's the harm? Then there's Phoebe here, I can't go without her. Not that I often clap eyes on the gal now that my lady has taken her into service. To be sure my lady gives her double wages, and odds and scraps of left-off finery she's too proud to wear. But if I were Phoebe and in her place I'd feather my nest with something better than muslin and ribbons. Only to hear Phoebe talk of my lady's jewels and treasures – why, one of them shiny things she showed me t'other day would set a man up for life.

Enter PHOEBE MARKS *up left. She is a fair haired girl in her early twenties with an interesting rather than pretty face. She is slim and fragile. She crosses to left of the seat.*

Phoebe *(taking* LUKE *by surprise)*: What. Luke?
Luke *(rising and retreating right centre)*: Hallo! Why it be Phoebe. You give me the shivers a comin' down so still and sudden.
Phoebe *(moving to left of* LUKE*)*: I can see the Lime Tree Walk from my bedroom window and when I saw you sitting here, I came at once to see you. Are you glad to see me, Luke?
Luke *(boorishly)*: Glad? Aye, I'm glad. Why do you want to know?

Phoebe: You don't seem as if you were glad. No one would think to look at your face that we were sweethearts.

Luke (*crossing her and sitting down on the seat again*): Course we be sweethearts. Ain't you bound in promise to me these six years? 'Tain't likely when I knows you've a good place that I'm going to be foolish enough to cry off. You've been rising in servitude of late. First you were housemaid, then parlour maid and now you be lady's maid – at the top of the servant tree, as you might say.

Phoebe (*sitting on* LUKE'S *right*) You might tell me if you think my journey abroad's improved me.

Luke (*picking up the wood and knife and continuing the whittling*): It ain't put any fresh colour in your cheeks, Phoebe. You used to be as plump as a pippin and as brown as a russet and now look at you – you be as thin as a yard of pump water.

Phoebe: But it's not genteel to be plump – so my lady says.

Luke (*with a hoarse laugh*): Genteel! Who wants you to be genteel? Not I for one.

Phoebe: But all the world is not of your opinion, Luke. I'd lots of pleasant things said to me when my lady and me was travelling abroad. Do you know, Luke, I learned more in the last three months abroad than I did in a year's schooling. What do you think, Luke? I can speak a little French now.

Luke: French! A deal of use that'll be to you when you're Mrs. Marks my wife instead of Miss Marks, my cousin. Dang me, Phoebe, I suppose when we've saved money enough between us to buy a bit of a farm, you'll be 'parley-vooing' to the cows.

Phoebe (*biting her lips and turning away*): What a fine thing it is for Miss Graham as was, to have a rich husband that thinks there isn't one spot on the earth that's good enough for her to set her foot upon.

Luke: 'Tain't every poor girl that is lucky enough to find an old fool of a rich baronet to marry her.

Phoebe: Sir Michael perfectly dotes on her. She has just as much money as she chooses to ask for.

Luke: Aye, it's a fine thing, Phoebe, to have lots of money, and I hope you'll be warned by that, my lass, to save up your money agen we get married.

Phoebe: Just look who be talking! Luke Marks, it be – who never does a day's work but skulks about from one public house to another all day long. I'm ashamed of you.

Luke: I'll reform when I marry you, Phoebe.

Phoebe: A poor prospect I'll have in marrying you, I'm afraid. Some folks has all the luck. Look at Lady Audley – what was she in Mr. Dawson's house only three months ago?

Luke: A governess – that's what her was.

Phoebe: Maybe – but she was only a servant like me – taking wages and working for them. You should have seen her shabby clothes, Luke – worn and patched and darned and turned and twisted, yet always looking nice upon her somehow. She gives me more as a lady's maid here than ever she got from Mr. Dawson as governess. And now look at her!

Luke: Why, I believe you be jealous of her.

Phoebe: Jealous – not I. I knows my place. Oh, but you should have seen her while we were abroad with a crowd of gentlemen always hanging about her. Sir Michael didn't mind one jot. He was only too proud to see her so admired. You should have seen her laugh and talk with them, throwing all their compliments and fine speeches back at them, as if they had been pelting her with roses. She set everybody mad about her wherever she went – her singing, her playing, her painting, her dancing, and her beautiful smile! She was always the talk of the place as long as we stayed in it.

Luke: Well, never mind her. Just you take care that you make hay while the sun shines. What would you say to a public house for you and me by and by, my girl? There be a great deal of money to be made out of a public house.

Phoebe (*rising and moving centre*): I don't know, Luke. It be such noisy work.

Luke: Pooh! It's cheerful – that's all and with a bit of cherry ribbon in your hat you wouldn't look too bad behind the bar.

Phoebe: Yes, but think of the money we should need.

Luke: The Castle Inn at Mount Stanning is in the market. If you were to speak to my lady, Sir Michael would put us up, I know.

Phoebe: Aye, she can do anything with him.

Luke: And you can do anything with her.

Phoebe: What do you mean, Luke?

Luke: I've heard you say as much. *(Rising and moving to* PHOEBE*)* Now Phoebe, one of them brilliants would buy the Castle and to spare.

Phoebe: Hush, Luke, how can you talk so?

Luke: Have you got any of them about you girl *(grabs her)*.

Phoebe: Don't, Luke, let me go. I did very wrong to let you see that bracelet. I shouldn't if you hadn't teased me so.

Luke: You said you would show me the house and the fine gildings and looking glasses and my lady's room. Are there more jewels there?

Phoebe: More? Why there's a box crammed with rubies and diamonds and emeralds and pearls, Luke, as big as – a pigeon's egg.

Luke: A pigeon's egg. I'd like to see them. Ain't you taking me round now, Phoebe?

Phoebe: No, not now, Luke. My lady's in. They are expecting company. Robert is coming down tomorrow.

Luke: What, the young 'counsillor' – him as is licensed to shoot the hen pheasants?

Phoebe: He's quite turned Miss Alicia's head has Mr. Robert.

Luke *(crossing* PHOEBE *and moving right)*: That's about all he can turn then for I've heard tell he's a poor hand at his trade.

Phoebe *(turning on* LUKE*)*: And who told you that, Luke Marks?

Luke *(by the well)*: I ain't a saying. I knows what I knows, I do. *(Bending down and picking up a bag)* Now, what's this I just found by the old well?

Phoebe *(moving to left of* LUKE*)*: Why if it isn't my lady's bag. She was sketching out here this morning. She must have left it. Give it to me, Luke.

Luke *(opening the bag)*: There ain't no harm in having a peep.

Phoebe *(trying to take the bag away)*: No, No!

Luke: Hum! Only a handkerchief and a card case. Wait a minute, though – what be this here – see this lump in the leather. There's an inside pocket and there be something in it.
Phoebe: Will you give me the bag, Luke – you've no right – what have you got there?
Luke *(who has taken a small packet from the bag)*: It's a sort of little packet. Something wrapped up in paper.
Phoebe: Give it to me – your great big dirty hands will soil it.
Luke *(opening the packet) (music cue 7 to end of scene)*: Why it be an old shoe – a baby's shoe and a bit of yellow hair.
Phoebe *(taking the packet and moving centre) (quietly)*: So this is what my lady hides in her bag.
Luke *(carelessly)*: I call it queer rubbish to keep in such a place.
Phoebe *(putting the packet into her pocket)*: You will bear witness where I found this, Luke?
Luke *(moving to* PHOEBE*)*: Why, you're never going to keep that? You be a fool, Phoebe.
Phoebe: Perhaps I am – perhaps I am. All the same, Luke, I'll tell you this. I'd rather have this little parcel than all the jewels in my lady's box.
Luke: What do you mean?
Phoebe: Never mind now. I'll tell you some other time.
Luke: What maggot is in your brain? What are you thinking of, gal?
Phoebe: What be I thinking, Luke? I'm thinking that you shall have your public house after all – never fear, you shall have it.

CURTAIN

ACT ONE
SCENE THREE

Music cue 8.

The library at Audley Court – later the same day. There is a window up centre and entrances up left and up right. A sofa stands, at an angle, stage left and an armchair down right. There is a desk up right centre with a chair behind it. The walls each side of the window are lined with books. When the curtain rises, ALICIA AUDLEY *is seated in the chair right. She is a dark-haired girl of* 19. LADY AUDLEY *is seated on the sofa. She is in her early twenties, small and pretty with dark hair in ringlets. She is sketching a small picture.*

Lady A *(looking up)*: Alicia.
Alicia: Yes, Lady Audley?
Lady A: Lady Audley! Your formality freezes me. Why not Lucy or at least Aunt?
Alicia: I don't know. It seems natural to –
Lady A: To reject my affection when I offer it. Well, perhaps it is for the best. Mr. Dawson used to say that acid and alkali won't combine.
Alicia *(bristling)*: You mean then, that I am –
Lady A: Come, let us not quarrel. I am well aware that you look upon me as an intruder. I'm sorry for it. In marrying Sir Michael, I never contemplated robbing you of a father's love.
Alicia: You could not if you would.
Lady A: It seems very hard that you cannot love me, Alicia, for I have never been used to making enemies. If we cannot be friends, let us at least be neutral. You will not try to injure me?
Alicia *(rising and moving to right of sofa)*: Injure you, Lady Audley? And how, pray, should I injure you?
Lady A: You'll not try to deprive me of your father's affection?
Alicia: I may not be as amiable as you are, my lady, and I may not have the same sweet smiles and pretty words for

every stranger I meet, but I am not capable of contemptible meanness; and even if I were, I think you are so secure in my father's love that nothing but your own act will ever deprive you of it.
Lady A *(aside)*: What can she mean by that? *(Aloud – with a little grimace)* What a severe creature you are, Alicia! I suppose you intend to infer by all that, that I am deceitful. Why, I can't help smiling at people, and speaking prettily to them. I know I'm no *better* than the rest of the world, but I can't help it if I'm *pleasanter* – it's constitutional. Well, I suppose I must use my influence with your cousin and try to get him to reconcile us.
Alicia *(moving away right)*: I've no doubt Mr. Robert Audley will be quite ready to listen to any argument of yours.
Lady A: I hope he will. Do you know, Alicia, I'm dying to see him. Something whispers to me that we shall be firm friends.
Alicia: Very likely. Bob Audley is too idle to make many enemies.
Lady A: Then we must do our very best to encourage his lazy habits. He shall have a hammock in the Lime Tree Walk and doze over his novels all day long. He's quite a curiosity, isn't he?
Alicia: In being curious about nothing – yes. He doesn't attempt to make himself useful.
Lady A: No matter so long as he does not make himself disagreeable.
Alicia: But here comes my father and Robert with him too. Now that's just like him when he wasn't expected until tomorrow – taking us by surprise.
Lady A: For my part, I like being taken by surprise.
Alicia *(returning to her chair) (aside)*: Now to scold him and make myself thoroughly objectionable.
Lady A *(aside)*: And now for a first impression. It would be a poor policy to make a foe of Sir Michael's favourite.

Music cue 9.

Enter SIR MICHAEL AUDLEY, *a tall man of* 65 *with a deep sonorous voice. He has a white beard. He is followed by* ROBERT AUDLEY.

Sir M *(taking hold of* ROBERT *and leading him to centre stage). (Moving to right of sofa) (music ends)*: Lucy, my love, let me introduce you to the poacher I encountered in Hazel Copse – he's unarmed.

Robert *(aside)*: But she's fully prepared and with the fatal panoply of Venus *(bows)*.

Sir M: My nephew, Robert Audley, Lucy. Barrister of the Southern Circuit – full of brains but short of briefs – eh, Bob?

Lady A: And panting, I've no doubt, for an opportunity of setting the Woolsack on fire. When I am attacked, Mr. Audley, I shall retain you as my champion.

Robert: In that case, my chance for a brief is, I fear, hopeless. *(Aside)* The idea of this fairy creature being my aunt. It's simply preposterous. *(Moving to* ALICIA *and speaking quietly to her)* What a smile! No wonder my uncle was caught – she is perfectly fascinating – charming!

Alicia *(to* ROBERT – *spitefully)*: I tell you she is a wax doll. But, of course, like all men, you are smitten with her at first sight.

Robert: Nonsense. What a jealous little girl you are, Alicia.

Sir M *(moving to centre stage)*: What are you two chattering about?

Robert: Nothing of any consequence, I assure you, uncle.

Lady A *(rising)*: Well, now that Mr. Audley –

Sir M: Mr. Audley? No, no – Bob, if you please. He's always Bob here.

Lady A: Well then Mr. Bob, where shall you be most at home, with your pipes and cigars? Where will you be least regretful of the luxury of Fig Tree Court? Shall it be the Blue Room, or the –

Sir M: Neither, my love. This eccentric fellow will insist in putting up at the village inn.

Lady A: But why?

Robert: The reason, Lady Audley, is because I can't persuade a very dear old friend of mine who has journeyed down here with me, to share your hospitality. It was owing to him that I was prevented from coming down a month ago. It is a sad story.

Sir M: Who is he, Bob? Do I know him?

Robert: No, uncle, and you would not have found the poor fellow very entertaining company, I fear, for his wife is lately dead and he has just returned from the Antipodes.

Lady A: Ah!

Sir M: Poor man; what is his name?

Robert: George Talboys.

Lady A (*aside – shuddering*): George Talboys! *Music cue* 10 (*short*).

Robert: It is useless trying to persuade him. Ever since his wife's death, he will –

Lady A (*recovering*): Oh, do not apologise, pray. We all appreciate your kind feelings. Your first duty is to your friend.

Robert: I can't desert George Talboys. If you knew, uncle, what the poor boy has suffered.

Lady A (*quickly*): Don't tell us, *please* don't tell us. I should dream of it. (*Moving in to* SIR MICHAEL) Shouldn't I, dearest?

Sir M: You mustn't frighten my little dove. But, Bob old boy, after your hot walk what do you say to a glass of sherry or some cider cup?

Lady A: Yes, do have some cider cup, Robert.

Sir M: And Alicia shall immortalize the brew with a sprig of burrage.

Robert: Culled by her own fair hands.

Alicia: It's a great deal more than you deserve, tantalizing one in this way.

Robert: Au revoir, my dear aunt. (*Moving to* ALICIA) Come, Alicia (*aside*) Hang me, if I don't begin to wish myself in my uncle's gouty slippers.

Sir M (*moving up left*): Come then. (*Exit*).

ROBERT *and* ALICIA *follow him to up left and exit. After they have gone,* LADY AUDLEY *moves to right and pulls the bell cord. She then moves down right centre.*

Music cue 11.

Lady A: He lives! George lives! What is more he is here, here in the village not a mile hence. Can he suspect? No, no, the notice in the paper must have allayed suspicion. Still – not a moment is to be lost. While he is here I cannot move – I dare not move for fear of certain exposure. (*End of music*).

Enter PHOEBE *up left*.
Phoebe, come here, child.

PHOEBE *moves to left of* LADY AUDLEY.

Phoebe: How pale you are, my lady. Are you ill?
Lady A: No, I feel a little tired – nothing more. Phoebe, have my trunks packed and all in readiness. I may have to go to London, tomorrow early.
Phoebe: But what of the party, my lady?
Lady A: Do as I bid.
Phoebe: But Sir Michael, my lady – does he know?
Lady A: Don't pester me with questions, child – he will be informed. I have trusted you; see that you don't abuse that confidence. Now go –
Phoebe: Only one moment. I want to speak to your ladyship about Marks.
Lady A: What of him?
Phoebe (*producing the packet from under her apron*): He found this, my lady – it had fallen out of your bag. *Music cue* 12 (*short*).
Lady A (*snatching the packet*): Give it to me. (*Aside*) Great Heavens, I shall be discovered! What am I to do?
Phoebe: Luke wants to marry me, you know, my lady.
Lady A: I see. And are you in love with him?
Phoebe: I don't think I can love him, but I promised years ago to be his wife. I don't think I can break that promise now.
Lady A: You shall not marry him. I cannot afford to part with you.
Phoebe: My good kind mistress, you don't know Luke Marks. 'Twill be my ruin if I break my word. I *must* marry him. Even when he was a boy he was always violent and revengeful. I saw him once take up a knife in a quarrel with his mother. My lady, I dare not refuse.

Lady A: You silly girl, you think he'd murder you, do you? What nonsense! If murder is in him do you think you would be any safer as his wife? If you thwarted him or made him jealous; if he wanted to marry another woman or to get hold of some pitiful bit of money of yours, couldn't he murder you then? No, Phoebe, I'll give him a few pounds and send him about his business.

Phoebe *(catching hold of* LADY AUDLEY'S *hands and clasping them convulsively – vehemently)*: My lady, don't ask me to thwart him. I tell you I must marry him. You don't know what he is. It will be my ruin if I break my word.

Lady A: Very well then, Phoebe. I shall be sorry to lose you but I have promised to stand your friend in all things. *(Aside)* Besides, I dare not refuse now that she has seen the contents of the packet. *(Aloud)* What does your cousin mean to do for a living when you are married?

Phoebe: He would like to take himself a public house.

Lady A: I see. Very well, he shall take a public house and the sooner he drinks himself to death the better for you and everybody. I'll speak to Sir Michael at once. And remember, Phoebe, have all prepared for tomorrow and do not mention it to anyone.

Phoebe *(moving up left)*: I'll not forget. *(With a sigh)* You are very good, my lady.

Lady A: Do not thank me.

Exit PHOEBE. LADY AUDLEY *moves left, picks up her bag from the sofa and puts away the packet.*

Music cue 13.

How could I have been so foolish as to leave the bag where its contents could be discovered? Until today every trace of the old life had melted away, every clue to identity buried and forgotten. I thought there would be no more dependence, no more drudgery, no more humiliations – and now – No, by heaven, I will do everything in my power to see that it remains so – nothing shall stand in my way – nothing! *Music ends.*

Enter SIR MICHAEL *up left. He moves to right of* LADY AUDLEY.

Sir M: Well, my love, I hope you are impressed by our nephew.
Lady A: His natural easy manner is quite refreshing – he's far too frank and open for a lawyer.
Sir M: Bob is a capital fellow, Lucy. I was sure you'd like him. It's a pity he can't induce his friend to take up his quarters with us.
Lady A: Perhaps it is for the best. Widowers, you know, are sad bores.
Sir M: A left-handed compliment for somebody, eh, Lucy?
Lady A: I mean till they are recaptured. It isn't everyone who has your courage, dear.
Sir M: Nor every woman of twenty the good nature to take pity on an old man, Lucy.
Lady A: Then you don't repent your bargain?
Sir M: You are the delight of my life – where'er you go you carry joy and brightness with you – all love, admire and praise you.
Lady A (*aside*): Perhaps if they knew me rightly they would curse me.
Sir M: You are the best and sweetest creature that ever lived, and I the most blessed of men in having won you to my wife. Would that I could have given you a kingdom with my love (*he draws her to him and presses his lips to her forehead*).
Lady A: Sir Michael, I have a favour to ask you on Phoebe's part. I am going to be very importunate. Let us talk it over in the other room.
Sir M: Very well, my dear. Come along. You know I can refuse you nothing –

They exit up right.

ALICIA *and* ROBERT *enter up left.* ALICIA *moves to the window and looks out.* ROBERT *stands on her left.*

Alicia: And so the tap room of the village inn has more charms for you than the society of Audley Court, eh?
Robert: How silly of you, Alicia. George would be ill at ease here. I dare say the cigar boxes will be empty and the fishing tackle broken by the end of the week.

Alicia: And Captain Talboys will lose the chance of seeing the most charming woman in Essex.
Robert: How you make a poor devil eat his words. You – you'd provoke a saint, Alicia.
Alicia: Little fear then of provoking you.
Robert: That's it – don't spare me. She is charming, you can't deny it, but she'd stand a poor chance of getting much admiration out of George. Poor fellow, his heart is in his wife's grave in Ventnor churchyard.

Bell.

Alicia: Ah, the dressing bell. Don't forget you must not run away without introducing me to your romantic friend.
Robert: I'll entice him over here some day and – what's the matter?
Alicia *(looking out of the window)*: Look – a stranger in the Lime Tree Walk.
Robert *(looking out)*: Why if it isn't George. Lost all patience I suppose – or lost his way. *(Moving to exit up left)* I'll have him in, if it's only to gratify your curiosity. *(Exit)*.
Alicia *(moving down centre)*: I vow, Robert seems quite taken with the wax doll. She is the first woman of whom I have ever heard him say a civil word. Suppose he was to fall in love with her? Oh, but that is out of the question. The idea is too preposterous. But it is a shame to tease him, he must have a very kind heart to bury himself in the back parlour of a country inn, when Audley Court is open to him. *(Moves right)*.
Robert *(entering up left with* GEORGE*)*: Come, come, just a peep at the old place and the young beauties. *(Moving to right of* ALICIA*)* My cousin Miss Audley – Captain Talboys.

GEORGE *bows and moves to left of* ROBERT.

Alicia: Won't you think better of your resolve, and dine with us, Captain Talboys? Sir Michael, I'm sure, would be delighted.
George: Thank you, you're very kind, but I'm not fit company for anybody – not even for Bob.
Robert: Much obliged to you for the compliment. No we must be back for our humble 'leg and trimmings'. *(To*

GEORGE) What do you think of the place, eh? Snug, isn't it? *(Moving above the sofa to an easel which holds a portrait standing at right angles to the audience on the left wall below the entrance)* Hallo, what's this, mysteriously swaddled in green baize?

Alicia *(moving to right of* GEORGE*)*: That's the portrait of the most charming woman in Essex. It's not quite finished yet but it's a most remarkable likeness.

Robert: Her portrait? By jove, that's lucky. *(To* GEORGE*)* Here come and look. If you're too shy to be presented to the original, we must at least introduce you to the copy. *(He throws back the cover as* GEORGE *goes up to his right)* We must have a light. *(Moves to the desk and picks up an oil lamp, returns to the right of* GEORGE *who is staring at the portrait).*

Music cue 14.

George *(aside)*: What is this? Her face! Hers! Good Heavens, what can this mean? It is the likeness of my wife! Some fearful mystery is here. Does she live to be the wife of Sir Michael Audley? Oh, for some means to be certain! Let me not be rash – not a word to Robert at present. I'll linger in the park and if I've been deceived by her – woe to the traitoress – woe, woe, woe – and punishment most dire! *(Rushes off up left). Music ends.*

Robert: George, where are you going? *(Moves up to exit left and looks off) (to* ALICIA*)* What can be the matter? He's got one of his gloomy fits. He's never been the same man since his wife's death.

Alicia: But how strange to run off like that, without a word.

Robert: I must be after him or he'll lose himself – so goodbye.

Alicia: Goodnight, Bob *(she moves to* ROBERT*).*

Robert: You will forgive me, Alicia?

Alicia: Forgive you, Robert?

Robert: Yes, it is not my fault if – if –

Alicia: If what?

Robert: If my aunt has the misfortune to be the most charming woman in Essex.

Alicia: Well! *(She crosses him and sweeps off indignantly).*

Robert: What can I have said to upset her? *(Exit).*

CURTAIN

ACT ONE
SCENE FOUR

Music cue 15.

The Lime Tree Walk – at dusk the same evening. LADY AUDLEY *enters right.*

Lady A: If I were not afraid, before tomorrow's sun has risen I'd have put miles between him and me. *(Moving to centre stage)* Afraid, did I say? No – courage! I'll be strong and brave. I have been brave to dare so much already and I'll not falter now. Were I to play the coward, I should lose all – yes, wealth, position, everything for which I've fought, everything for which I've suffered. *(Moving left)* And then there is Phoebe. I cannot tell her this; she knows too much already. I must fight my way alone. How did he know Sir Michael's nephew? I never heard him mention his name. *(There is a noise up right)* Who's there?
George *(stepping from behind the well up right)*: Your husband, Helen Talboys – your husband!

LADY AUDLEY *starts to move away left but* GEORGE *rushes across and catches hold of her.*

Wait, woman, devil or what you are – you have much to answer for before you leave this spot.
Lady A *(breaking free)*: Hold! Let us endeavour to commence calmly.
George: Calmly! Are you not my wife who swore to honour me and love me and obey me till –
Lady A: Death did us part. I did. I kept my word, George Talboys. You abandoned me. You, of your own free will were dead to me. You left me in poverty.
George: No – 'tis false. You know it. I but fled from you in the hope that I might return and make you wealthy.
Lady A: You lie! You left me with no better protector than a drunken father and the burden of a helpless child who, lying in his cradle, seemed, with his baby smiles to mock the memory of his father. Thank heavens, he was spared his mother's sufferings.

George: What do you mean?

Lady A: Alas, he is dead!

George *(moving away right – aside)*: Dead! My son dead! And I have toiled and suffered for this woman. *(Aloud)* What have I done to you that my reward should be this grevious wrong?

Lady A *(moving to him)*: Wrong! Have *you* not wronged *me*? Listen to me. After your departure, I vainly sought employment – a wife whom her husband has deserted could not be innocent of all fault. I was penniless. Before me was starvation or a repulsive life of infamy. I changed my name and became Miss Lucy Graham. I entered the family of a gentleman as governess to his daughters. There I was seen, admired and loved by Sir Michael. He offered me his hand. Weary of poverty and drudgery, fixed in the belief that you would never return to claim me, I became his wife.

George: Oh, infamy! Infamy indeed!

Lady A: Scarcely was I married when your letter reached me, telling me you were about to quit Australia, and naming the time when I might expect to behold you. What did I do then? Did I groan and tear my hair? No – I caused to be inserted in the papers the announcement of my own death, and if you have visited the grave, you have seen the words 'Helen Talboys' written on its tombstone.

George *(aside)*: Oh, horrible! This, the woman I have so wildly loved, has, wantonly, for her own selfish ends, driven me to despair.

Lady A: The past cannot be recalled. The wealth and splendour I have attained I will not lose. Do you think I will be cast down by you, George Talboys? No, I will conquer you or I will die!

George: And what means will you take to conquer me? What power will you employ to silence me?

Lady A: I will do anything rather than go back to my old life. *(Moving away left)* I tell you what I will do. You shall share the riches at my command. I will give you gold.

George *(moving to centre stage)*: Gold! Gold purchased by

"*What are you thinking of, gal?*"
LUKE *and* PHOEBE MARKS
Act I, Scene II

"*She is perfectly fascinating*"
LADY AUDLEY, SIR MICHAEL,
ROBERT *and* ALICIA

Act I, Scene III

"—*the very last service. Die! Die!*"
GEORGE TALBOYS *and* LADY AUDLEY
Act I, Scene IV

your falsehood! You offer me wealth. I am worth twenty thousand pounds. 'Twas all for you – for you! And now you – no, no, false woman, I seek not a bribe.
Lady A: Is it then revenge that you seek?
George: No – not revenge, but justice! *(Moving to her)* I will never forgive you for the lie that has broken my heart. You have plucked it from my breast, have trampled upon it and now – now I have no heart in which to feel one sentiment of mercy for you. I would have forgiven any wrong but that one deliberate and passionless wrong that you have done me. No power on earth shall turn me from my purpose to take you to the man you have deceived and force you to tell your terrible, wicked story.
Lady A: You will turn informer then?
George: No, not informer – but I am determined that you shall be punished – punished for your dreadful wrongs.
Lady A *(with a sardonic smile)*: Then you will war with a woman?
George: To the death!
Lady A *(aside)*: Death! Death! Aye, that is the word. That is now the only method of escape – death! *(Aloud)* Then you are merciless –
George: As you are crafty. Last night the luxurious mansion of Audley Court sheltered you – tonight a prison's roof will cover your head.
Lady A *(crossing him to up centre)*: I defy you! I scorn you! I spurn you for a vindictive fool. Go to Sir Michael, if you will – denounce me do – and I will swear to him that you are a liar – a madman. He will believe me before you – he worships me blindly. I have gained his heart, his soul, his unbounded confidence, and before there is the felon's dock for me there shall be the maniac's cell for you. *(Laughing)* What think you now, George Talboys?
George: If there was but one witness of your identity, and that witness were removed from Audley Court by the width of the whole earth, I would bring him here to swear your identity and to denounce you. Your infamous cunning shall

no longer avail you, by Heaven!
Lady A *(aside)*: My cunning! He speaks truth indeed. Now that all else has failed me it is that I must now employ if I am to escape this situation. *(Aloud)* Farewell, George Talboys *(she starts to go)*.
George *(moving up and grabbing her by the wrist)*: You go not yet.
Lady A *(shaking him off)*: You have bruised my wrist. *(Aside)* Now have I a plan that will rid me of him for ever. *(Aloud)* But one moment. I will accompany you if you will let me have a few seconds to myself so that I can calm my nerves before the ordeal I must suffer when I come face to face with Sir Michael.
George: Very well – but a few seconds – that is all. Be quick.
Music cue 16 to end of the act.
Lady A: I will.
TALBOYS *moves left and looks offstage. While his back is turned,* LADY AUDLEY *goes to the well, takes off the iron handle and conceals it in her right hand behind her back. (Aside)*
It is mine! That is one point gained – now for the second. *(Moves centre stage, feigning faintness)* Water, water, for mercy sake! *(She collapses on to the seat)* My head burns like fire.
George *(crossing to her)*: This is some trick to escape me – but I will not leave you.
Lady A: I do not wish you to. *(Gives him a white handkerchief)* Stoop down and dip this in the bucket in that well over there. I can then bathe my throbbing temple.
GEORGE *takes the handkershief and goes to the well.*
George: It is the last service I shall render you.
Lady A: *(creeping up behind him)* It is indeed – the very last service! *(striking him on the head with the iron handle)* Die! Die! *(She pushes him down the well)* He is gone! He is gone! *(To centre stage)* And no one was witness to the deed. *(Exulting)* Dead men tell no tales! I am free! I am free! I am free!
She raises her arms in triumph and laughs wildly as

THE CURTAIN FALLS
ON ACT ONE

ACT TWO
SCENE ONE

The library at Audley Court – twelve months later. ROBERT *is seated at the desk reading a newspaper.*

Robert *(reading)*: "Mr. George Talboys – Any person who has met this gentleman since the 7th inst., or who can furnish any information respecting his movements subsequent to that date, will be liberally rewarded on communicating with A.Z. 14 Chancery Lane." A year gone since that advertisement was first inserted. A year gone in trying to fathom the mystery of his disappearance. A year gone and still no tidings! Should I be justified in letting the chain which I have slowly put together, link by link, drop at this point? Or must I go on adding fresh links to that fatal chain until the last rivet falls into place and the circle is complete? I think and believe that I shall never see my friend's face again, and that no exertion of mine can ever be of any benefit to him. In plainer, harder words, I believe him to be dead. Am I bound to discover how and where he died? Or being, as I think, on the road to that discovery, shall I do a wrong to the memory of George Talboys by turning back or stopping still? Then Sir Michael, my uncle – must I bring dishonour and disgrace on him? No, I must not hesitate – it is too late to turn back. Heaven help those who stand between me and the secret for they will be sacrificed to the memory of George Talboys.

Enter LADY AUDLEY *up left.*

Justice to the dead first – mercy to the living afterwards!
Lady A *(moving to left of the desk)*: All alone, Robert? Well, you seem satisfied with your company.
Robert *(rising)*: Eh?
Lady A: Yes, you were chattering to yourself most energetically.
Robert: Was I? The effect, I suppose of –
Lady A: Those bad habits you contract in Chambers. Your life in the Temple must be a very mysterious one.
Robert: You are right, Lady Audley. It is full of mysteries – at least to me.

Lady A *(moving down left)*: Now, please, Robert, please, don't talk about it in that uncomfortable manner, but try and fancy this is Fig Tree Court and make yourself at home. Don't be afraid, I don't mind your Cabanas *(sits on right end of sofa)*.

Robert *(picking up a box from the desk and taking out a cigar)*: You are very good. You are quite sure the smoke won't annoy you?

Lady A: Oh no indeed. (ROBERT *lights his cigar*) You are a droll, eccentric creature, Robert. Do you know that you puzzle me sometimes?

Robert: Do I?

Lady A: Yes. You are obsessed with that phantom friend of yours who went off in that most unceremonious way. Mr. – Mr. – what was his name?

Robert *(moving right)*: George Talboys.

Lady A: To be sure. I have thought more about your friend than you would give me credit for. I daresay his wife's death prayed upon his mind.

Robert: No doubt.

Lady A: Anyway, now that he is dead beyond doubt, I should –

Robert: How do you know he is dead beyond doubt? *(Moves to her right)*.

Lady A: Dear me, how you do take a poor little woman up, to be sure – just like you lawyers. What I mean is that now that he has disappeared you have become quite a different man. You'll wear yourself out, if you go on in this way. You have been half round England, I believe, in search of him.

Robert: I'd go round the world, Lady Audley, to try to find George Talboys – or his grave. There is not a seaport on our coasts where I am not known, nor an underwriter at Lloyds, or a shipbroker's clerk who doesn't curse me for a meddling, curious fellow. At one time I had hopes of success in Yorkshire, and again I thought Southampton might enlighten me.

Lady A *(after a pause)*: And what do you infer from all this?

Robert *(moving away right)*: First that George never went beyond Southampton at all.

Lady A: Really? But you told me once that you had traced him there. You told me that you had seen his father-in-law and more, that his father-in-law had seen him.

Robert: True, but I've reason to doubt that gentleman's integrity.

Lady A: Good gracious me! What do you mean by all this?

Robert (*moving to below the desk*): Have you ever studied any works on evidence, Lady Audley? I suppose not – I have. That study has made me determined to discredit the words of any man or woman unless confirmed by proofs.

Lady A: Indeed! Then the sooner you discard those views the better, Robert Audley.

Robert (*sitting on the downstage end of the desk*): Hear me out, please. Sir Michael may have told you that I have never practised as a barrister. I have shrunk from my duties as I have from all the fatigues of this troublesome life but we are sometimes forced into the very position we have most avoided. And I have, of late, found myself compelled to turn my attention to the study of the criminal law.

Lady A: Dear me, you are quite a detective. I wonder with your suspicious tendencies you haven't enrolled yourself at Scotland Yard.

Robert: I wish I had, Lady Audley, rather than to have entered my uncle's house during the past year.

Lady A: If you will insist in talking in enigmas, you must excuse me if I fail to understand you.

Robert (*rising and moving down to the right of the sofa*): Let me try to make myself plain. George Talboys –

Lady A (*rising and moving down left*): My dear Robert, you are a bore. Can't you find any other subject for conversation?

Robert: Not so fitting for the present season, Lady Audley. Listen – a year has elapsed since the insertion of my advertisement.

Lady A: I am unlikely to forget. It was at the head of the second column of *The Times* all last season – and it has resulted in nothing.

Robert: Pardon me. It has resulted in the belief of my friend's death and –

Lady A: Exactly as I told you – but what more?

Robert: In the consequent examination of the effects he left in my chamber.

Lady A: Indeed – and they are, I suppose, coats, waistcoats, varnished boots and meerschaum pipes.

Rober *(moving to* LADY AUDLEY*)*: And letters, Lady Audley – letters.

Lady A: Of course. The usual rubbish sanctified by time – heap of old letters from old school fellows, his brother officers –

Robert *(moving closer to* LADY AUDLEY*)*: And his wife!

Lady A: His wife? And you've been amusing yourself with laughing over those amatory platitudes? Oh, fie, Mr. Audley, fie!

Robert: I have done no such thing – the seal upon the string remains unbroken. Talking of letters, – what a pretty hand you write, Lady Audley.

Lady A: Do I? You know my handwriting then?

Robert: Yes, I know it very well – very well indeed. I should know it among a thousand.

Lady A: Now, take my advice, Robert, and shake off this morbid fancy by change of air and scene. Take a nice long trip on the continent.

Robert: For my own sake I wish I could but I must stay where my duty bids me.

Lady A: And that is?

Robert *(moving to centre stage)*: Here in this house, or if my society is distasteful – in the neighbourhood.

Lady A: Because Sir Michael has not been so well of late, you mean – very natural. Your devotion does you credit.

Robert: There is no one to whom my uncle's life can be of more value than you, Lady Audley. Your happiness, your prosperity – in a word your safety depends on his existence.

Lady A: Yes, I know that as well as you. At his death envy and malice must be my position. *(Moving to left of* ROBERT*)* But while he lives, those who strike me must strike through him. And now, I must ask you to excuse me.

Robert: I take it, Lady Audley, you are asking me to leave this room. Very well, I will go, but before I do I have one further observation to make to you. The radius narrows every day. I am certain of one thing now – quite certain. George Talboys never left Audley Court. *(Moving up to exit right) (and turning to face* LADY AUDLEY*)* Lady Audley, listen to me, listen to me and listen well. I have given you fair warning. At our next meeting it must be justice and no pity. *(Exit)*.

Music cue 17.

Lady A *(moving down centre)*: Closer and closer around me seems to draw the circle, which threatens to bind me within its folds. Shall I yield to his menaces, and leave rank, wealth and position because he merely suspects me? No, my motto has, hitherto, been death or victory; and to that end am I fixed. He shall not remain here – no, not while I am mistress of this house. I'll speak to Sir Michael at once, he can refuse me nothing; and Alicia's jealousy will but seem to aid my purpose. Stay – those letters of which he spoke! I could defy him if they were once in my possession. I must think of a way of obtaining them. But my first action must be to have him removed from Audley Court. *(Moves down left)*.

End of music.

SIR MICHAEL *and* ALICIA *enter up left and move centre.*

Ah, my dear Sir Michael – my dear Alicia. I have been so lonely without you. *(Sits on left side of sofa)*.

Alicia: Not very lonely, I should think, when my cousin Robert has been with you *(aside to* SIR MICHAEL*)* He's smitten with her. I know he is.

Sir M *(aside)*: What the deuce does the girl mean? *(Aloud)* Can't my nephew speak to my wife without all this hubbub?

Alicia: It depends upon what subject he speaks.

Lady A *(aside)*: An excellent idea. I'll work on it.

Sir M: And pray, my dear, do you think my nephew would be so ungentlemanly as to speak upon any subjects to Lady Audley, except those of duty and respect?

Alicia: I know he's struck with her, Father, and she with him.

Sir M *(moving to right of sofa)*: Lady Audley, you hear what this

silly, jealous girl says? Pray set her doubts at rest.
Lady A *(sighing)*: I wish I could. I fear he must leave here, Sir Michael.
Sir M: Is it that you are getting bored with his lazy habits, lying about on the damask ottoman as if he were at his club? Or is it his cigars, perhaps?
Lady A: Oh, no, no, it isn't that exactly. The fact is – dearest, you won't be angry if I speak plainly – Mr. Audley is a very agreeable young man, and a very honourable young man. But you know, Sir Michael, I am rather a young aunt for such a nephew and I think it would be better – much better – if Mr. Robert left here at once. I feel embarrassed in his presence and –
Sir M: And shall be no longer. He shall go tonight, Lucy! I've been a blind neglectful fool not to have thought of this before. My lovely little darling, it was scarcely just to Bob to expose the poor lad to your fascinations. I know him to be as good and truehearted a fellow as ever breathed but – but – he shall go tonight. Alicia my dear, kindly ring for a servant.

ALICIA crosses to the bell cord and pulls it. LADY AUDLEY *rises and goes to* SIR MICHAEL.

Lady A: My dear, kind considerate old angel *(kisses his cheek)* I love you more and more every day. *(To* ALICIA*)* And you, my poor girl, how shamefully has Robert treated you. *(Crossing* SIR MICHAEL *to centre)* Come with me *(holding out her hand)* I'll tell you such things about him, that will, I'm sure prevent you ever speaking to him again.
Alicia *(weeping)*: Oh, the false, deceitful, perfidious, perjured profligate.
Lady A *(putting her arm around* ALICIA*)* Dry your tears, my dear; he is not worth thinking about. Send him away at once, Sir Michael. Of all the things in the world, I hate hypocrisy the most. *(Leading* ALICIA *up left)* Come, my dear, come. Forget the base fellow, forget him.
Alicia: I will – I will – the artful crocodile!
Lady A *(aside)*: Well, Robert Audley – you have shown your hand and, thanks to your stupid courtesy, you have shown me

how to win the game. (*Exit with* ALICIA).

After they have gone out, SIR MICHAEL *goes to the desk and sits. Enter* MARTIN, *a parlourmaid, up left.*

Martin: You rang, sir?
Sir M: Yes, Martin, I did. Please find Mr. Robert Audley for me and ask him if he would be so good as to give me a few moments of his valuable time.
Martin: Very good, sir. I believe he is in the drawing room, sir. I'll go and ask him at once.
Sir M: Thank you, Martin.

Exit MARTIN *up left.*

Sir M: Now if I were like some husbands, I should be jealous of this precious nephew of mine; but with a woman like Lady Audley, I am so sure of my family honour remaining pure and unsullied, that I can lay comfort to my heart, and hold her up as a paragon of goodness to all the world.

Enter ROBERT *up left.*

Robert: You wish to speak to me, uncle?
Sir M: Yes, Robert. I will come straight to the point. I wish you to go tonight.
Robert (*moving to the left of the desk*): To London?
Sir M: Well – to leave here at any rate. It will be better for all concerned, believe me.
Robert: What is the matter? You look disturbed. Has anything unpleasant occurred? How can I serve you?
Sir M (*rising*): By doing as I have requested. My honour, my peace demand your absence from here at once, nephew. I will write to you and explain my meaning more fully.
Robert: God forbid that I should ever bring trouble upon such a noble heart as yours. God forbid that the lightest shadow of dishonour should ever fall upon your honoured head – least of all through any agency of mine.
Sir M: No more – no more I pray, but obey me (*moving up right*) Obey me! *Exit up right.*
Robert (*coming down centre*): This is strange. Ah, I compre-

hend. This is Lady Audley's work. She has been influencing my uncle against me. I will go – but I will not go far. No – I will be near at hand to watch my lady and, if needs be to show her to the world in her true colours.

Music cue 18.

CURTAIN

ACT TWO
SCENE TWO

The Lime Tree Walk – fifteen minutes later. ALICIA *is seated on the garden seat. She is reading a novel.* ROBERT *enters right.* ALICIA *continues to read.*

Robert *(moving to right of* ALICIA*)*: What are you reading there, Alicia?
Alicia: 'Changes and Chances'.
Robert: A novel?
Alicia: Yes.
Robert: Who is it by?
Alicia: The author of 'Follies and Faults'.
Robert: Is it interesting?
Alicia: Not particularly.
Robert: Instructive?
Alicia: Quite the reverse.
Robert: In that case, as I'm off very soon, perhaps you'll condescend to give me five minutes of your society.
Alicia: My father was quite right to ask you to go, Bob. I'm very glad you're going.
Robert: The deuce you are?
Alicia: You're doing no good here, Bob. You're fit for nothing now but to hold a skein of silk, or to read Tennyson to Lady Audley.
Robert *(imploringly)*: My dear, hasty impetuous Alicia, don't be so violent. Lady Audley interests me – strongly, strangely interests me and my uncle's country friends do not. That is my reason for courting her company – is that a sufficient reason, Alicia?
Alicia *(with a scornful toss of the head)*: It's as good an answer as I shall ever get from you, Bob.
Robert: Now don't be angry. We have not much time left for quarelling.
Alicia: Where shall you stay when you have left here?
Robert: I shan't be far off.
Alicia: At the Audley Arms, I suppose.

Robert: No – not at the Audley Arms but – in the neighbourhood.
Alicia *(aside)*: He cannot tear himself from her.
Robert: I wish to be within hail. Your father, Alicia, is far from well. I fear he is badly broken.
Alicia *(aside)*: He is playing the hypocrite *(aloud)* You think Papa altered?
Robert *(moving away right)*: Altered? He is breaking fast. If anything should happen to him I should wish to be near Audley Court ready to hold out the hand of aid and sympathy.
Alicia: That is very considerate of you.
Robert: I am anxious to give you my best advice. Don't be in a hurry to run off with the first fox-hunting baronet who comes your way, if you like any one else better. If you'll only be patient and take life easily and try to reform yourself of banging doors, bouncing in and out of rooms, talking of the stables, and riding across country, I've no doubt the person you prefer will, in the end, make you a very excellent husband.
Alicia *(with embarrassed indignation)*: Thank you, cousin, but as you may not know the person I prefer, perhaps you'd better not take it upon yourself to answer for him or me.

Music cue 19.

Robert *(moving to centre stage before speaking)*: No, to be sure. Of course, if I don't know him – but I thought I did.
Alicia *(rising and moving away left – violently)*: Did you! *(Aside)* Could it be that he does love her? No – he dare not love her! *(She begins to cry)*.
Robert *(going to her)*: Alicia, my darling, what is the matter?
Alicia: It's – it's – the feather of my hat that got into my eyes *(she crosses him and runs to the exit up right)* Goodbye, Bob, goodbye. *(Aside)* In love with her – I won't believe it. *(Exit)*. *End of music.*
Robert *(alone)*: What does all this mean? To fly at a fellow like that, without the least provocation! Woman is a riddle – a riddle that we have not yet solved.

Enter LADY AUDLEY *from up right. She moves to* ROBERT *down left.*

Lady A: Robert Audley, are you still here? I understood from Sir Michael that he had given you instructions to leave this house.

Robert: That is true, Lady Audley – very true. I was about to make my departure. This, I take it, is of your making?

Lady A *(laughing)*: You thought to triumph over me, Robert Audley, but you see now that I hold all the trump cards.

Robert: Indeed, Lady Audley – indeed. I gave you fair warning and it is your own folly which is to blame if I no longer spare you.

Lady A *(moving away right)*: I do not have to stand here and listen to your insults, Mr. Audley.

Robert: I think that you do, Lady Audley. *(Crossing to her)* You are trembling. Are you nervous?

Lady A: Yes, dreadfully nervous. I am worth a fortune to poor Mr. Dawson, the surgeon. He is always sending me camphor and sal volatile – but he can't cure me.

Robert: Do you remember what Macbeth tells his physician, my lady? Mr. Dawson may be far cleverer than the Scottish leach, but I doubt if even he can minister to the mind that is diseased. *Music cue 20 (short).*

Lady A *(turning on* ROBERT, *with eyes flashing)*: Who said that my mind was diseased?

Robert: I say so, my lady. Heaven knows that I wish to be merciful – that I would spare you as far as it is in my power to do so while doing justice to others – but justice must be done. Shall I tell you why you are nervous in this house, my lady?

Lady A *(with a laugh)*: If you can.

Robert: Because, for you, this house is haunted.

Lady A: Haunted?

Robert: Yes, haunted by the ghost of George Talboys.

Lady A: Why do you continue to torment me about this George Talboys? What is he to me?

Robert: He was a stranger to you, my lady, was he not?

Lady A: Of course – what should he be but a stranger? *(Crossing* ROBERT *and moving upstage centre)* I wish to know nothing of your friend. *(Turning to face* ROBERT*)* If he is dead, I am sorry for him. If he lives I have no further wish to see him or hear of him. *(Moving towards exit up right)* Now, I wish to go in to see my husband, if you don't mind, Mr. Audley. Please do not detain me any longer.

Robert *(going up to her left)*: Wait, Lady Audley. You will stay until you have heard what I have to say.

Lady A *(moving down left to the seat)*: Very well. Pray lose no time in saying it. *(Sits left end of seat)*.

Robert *(coming to centre stage)*: Lady Audley, I now believe the announcement in the newspapers of his wife's death, which struck my poor friend to the heart to have been a black and bitter lie, a base and cowardly blow in the dark. *(Moving to right of seat)* It was a treacherous dagger-thrust of an infamous assassin.

Lady A: Indeed! And what reason could anyone have had for announcing the death of Mrs. Talboys if she had been alive?

Robert *(quietly)*: The lady herself might have had a reason.

Lady A: What reason?

Robert: How if she had taken advantage of George's absence to win a richer husband? How if she had married again and wished to throw my poor friend off the scent by this false announcement?

Lady A *(shrugging her shoulders)*: Your suppositions are rather ridiculous, Mr. Audley. It is to be hoped that you have some reasonable grounds for them.

Robert: I have. The evidence I have collected against her wants only one link to be strong enough for her condemnation – and that link shall be added. I will spare no trouble in completing the chain, unless –

Lady A: Unless what?

Robert: Unless the woman I wish to save from degradation and punishment accepts the mercy I offer her, and takes warning while there is still time.

Lady A: She would be a very foolish woman if she suffered herself to be influenced by any such absurdity. Helen Talboys is dead. *The Times* newspaper declares she is dead. Her own father tells you that she is dead. *(Rising)* By what right do you come to me and torment me about George Talboys? By what right do you dare to say that she is still alive?

Robert: By the right of circumstantial evidence, Lady Audley.

Lady A: What circumstantial evidence?

Robert: When Helen Talboys left her father's house, she left a letter behind her – a letter in which she declared that she was weary of her old life, and that she wished to seek a new home and a new fortune. That letter is in my possession.

Lady A *(looking* ROBERT *straight in the eyes)*: Indeed!

Robert: Do you know whose handwriting resembles that of Helen Talboys so closely that the most dexterous expert could perceive no distinction between the two?

Lady A *(carelessly)*: A resemblance between the handwriting of two women is no very uncommon circumstance nowadays. You cannot deny the fact of Helen Talboy's death on the grounds that her handwriting resembles that of some surviving person.

Robert: But if a series of such coincidences lead up to the same point, what of that? Helen Talboys left her father's house, according to the declaration in her own handwriting, because she was weary of her old life, and wished to begin a new one. Do you know what I infer from this?

Lady A *(shrugging her shoulders)*: I have not the least idea.

Robert *(sternly)*: Lady Audley, defiance will not serve you. *(Moving close to her)* I have dealt fairly with you, and have given you ample warning. I gave you indirect notice of your danger less than an hour ago. You did not choose to take that warning but instead, persuaded your husband that I should be sent from this house. The time has come when I must speak plainly to you. Helen Talboys disappeared on the 16th August 1854 and upon the 17th of that month reappeared as Lucy Graham, the friendless girl, who undertook a profitless duty in consideration of a home in which she was asked no questions.

Lady A: You are mad, Mr. Audley. You are mad and my

husband shall protect me from your insolence *(sweeping past* ROBERT *to centre stage before turning to speak to him)*. What if this Helen Talboys ran away from her home upon one day, and I entered my employer's house upon the next – what does that prove? Nothing! Nothing! If you choose to insist that I am Helen Talboys you may – I shall not attempt to hinder you.
Robert: Then you will be able to bring someone forward who can identify you with the past?
Lady A: If I were placed in the criminal dock, I could, no doubt. But I am not in a criminal dock, Mr. Audley, and I do not choose to do anything but laugh at your ridiculous folly.
Robert *(moving to her)*: It is to be a duel to the death, then, my lady? You refuse to accept my warning? You choose to remain here and defy me?
Lady A: I do. *(Looking him full in the face)* It is no fault of mine if my husband's nephew goes mad and chooses me for the victim of his monomania.
Robert: So be it then, my lady. My friend George Talboys was last seen alive here in Lime Tree Walk. He was seen by a servant to enter these gardens but he was never seen to leave them. I believe that he never did leave them and that his body lies hidden in some forgotten corner of this place. I will have such a search made as will level this house to the ground, and root up every tree in these gardens, rather than I will fail to find the grave of my murdered friend.

Music cue 21 to end of scene.

Lady A *(moving away right – wildly)*: Ah! You shall never live to do this. I will kill you first. Why have you tormented me so? Why could you not let me alone? What harm have I ever done you, that you should make yourself my persecutor, and dog my steps, and watch my looks, and play the spy upon me? Do you want to drive me mad? Do you know what it is to wrestle with a mad woman? No! *(Laughing wildly)* No, you do not or you would never even – *(stopping abruptly and drawing herself up)* Go away, Mr. Audley. *(Changing her tone)* You are mad, I tell you. You are mad.
Robert *(moving up centre)*: I am going, my lady. *(Turning)* I

"*Good heavens, what can this mean?*"
ALICIA, ROBERT *and* GEORGE
Act I, Scene III

"*That question will be answered when you stand upon the scaffold, murderess!*"
ROBERT *and* LADY AUDLEY
Act II, Scene II

"*I know the value of her kindness!*"
PHOEBE, LUKE *and* LADY AUDLEY
Act II, Scene III

THE CLOSING MOMENTS OF THE PLAY

would have condoned your crimes out of pity to your wretchedness. You have refused to accept my mercy. I wished to have pity on the living. Henceforth I shall only remember my duty to the dead. *(Moves to exit up right).*
Lady A: What will you do? What need I to fear from one who has lost his wits. *(Moves to below seat – defiantly)* What will you do?
Robert: That question will be answered when you stand upon the scaffold, murderess! *(Exit).*

<small>LADY AUDLEY</small> *utters a wild shriek of agony, presses her hand to her heart, staggers back and falls senseless to the ground.*

CURTAIN

ACT TWO
SCENE THREE

The Castle Inn at Mount Stanning, the same night. There is a wooden table centre stage with a wooden settle upstage of it and a chair to left and right of it. Two candles are burning on the table. When the curtain rises LUKE *is seated above the table drinking from a tankard.* PHOEBE *is standing left. She is crying.*

Luke: What are you weeping for? I tell you that fellow in the other room won't budge. I've near soaked him in rum but it's no go. I tell you he won't give up possession without the money.

Phoebe: But what are we to do, Luke? Where's the money to come from?

Luke: Why from the same place – the same place it did before. I'll not be turned out of house and home for a – for a –

Phoebe: Hush! Hush! You're not sober. You don't know what you're saying.

Luke: I'm not so drunk as that, don't think it.

Phoebe: I told my lady of our distress when I called to see her today and she promised to help us.

Luke: And she shall keep her promise – you mark my words.

Phoebe: Do you know how much she's done for us already Luke – how kind she's been to us?

Luke: She's been kind, has she? *(With a drunken chuckle)* Thank her for nothing. I know the value of her kindness. She'd be uncommon kind, I daresay, if she wasn't obligated to be it. She won't get no snivelling gratitude out of me, I can tell you.

Phoebe *(sitting left of table)*: My lady has promised to settle the business for us. If we could only get rid of this place, Luke – sell the goodwill and –

Luke: Goodwill! *(Laughing)* The goodwill of this rotten, ramshackle shed of a paltry inn. What would that fetch without my lady's secret, eh? Tell me that.

Phoebe: Hush! Hush! When my lady has been so kind.

Luke: Kind? You don't seem to believe me, but I tell you,

I could bring my lady down on her marrow bones afore me if I liked. Aye, afore me – Luke Marks – the drunkard, the scamp and the idler – as folks call him. And I could do it without help of that old shoe and that bit of hair – I tell you. I knows what I knows and it be worth a fortune, I tell you *(finger to side of nose)*.
Phoebe: I don't know what you mean, Luke.
Luke: No – nor be ever likely to know what's more. *(Finger to side of nose)* I knows what I knows and I'll not share my secret with even you, my girl.
Phoebe *(rising)*: Hush, I hear a footstep. There's somebody at the wicket.
Luke: Another cursed bailiff, I'll be bound. Go and see who it is. If it's a customer there's not much for him – scarce a gallon left.
Phoebe: I'll go and see who it is *(exit left)*.
Luke *(alone)*: Well – we've made a pretty penny out of Phoebe's secret – now we'll have to see what mine will fetch.

Enter PHOEBE *left followed by* ROBERT. *She moves to left of the table,* ROBERT *on her left.*

Phoebe: It's Mr. Audley.
Luke: Huh! *(Aside)* What does he want at this time? *(Aloud)* Servant, Mr. Audley, Sir.
Robert: I've a favour to ask of you, Mr. Marks, and of your good wife – the favour of a bed and board for a few days.
Luke: You're welcome, Mr. Audley – most welcome – as long as you pay. Why have you left the Hall?
Robert: There is a little difference between my uncle and myself, but I don't want to leave the neighbourhood for a few days.
Phoebe: It will be very humble, Mr. Audley.
Robert: No matter. Humble and honest is better any day than fine fare and falsehood.
Phoebe: I'll make you as comfortable as I can, depend on it, sir. I'll go now and get the room ready. *(Exit right)*.
Robert: Luke, you shall join me in a mug of ale. You'll find that to your palate, I reckon. *(Moves to left of table)*.

Luke: Ecod! You reckon right. Since I've been landlord here I've had ale for breakfast, ale for lunch, ale for dinner, ale for tea and ale for supper.
Robert: You'll drink away all your profits, Luke.
Luke: A straw for the profits. I don't depend on this place to keep me but upon what I knows.
Robert *(aside)*: What can he mean? Does he know something that would be of advantage to me in my search for the truth, I wonder. *(Aloud)* Tell me your secret, Luke and I will give you ten guineas.
Luke: Tell you my secret for ten guineas when I can likely get a hundred or more for keeping it – not likely.
Robert: But suppose that you should be made to tell it.
Luke: Made? Who can do that? Not you. Brag is a good dog but Holdfast is better.
Robert *(aside)*: I see that soft words will go farther with this fellow than hard ones. I will ply him with drinks. Perhaps, that way I may get it out of him. *(Aloud)* Come, let us have that ale. *(Sits in chair left of table)* I'll pay for all we have tonight.
Luke: Then you are a true Briton. A gentleman like you will always be welcome. *(Rising, moving to right and calling off)* Phoebe! Phoebe! Draw a quart of ale from the third barrel *(returning to table and sitting right)* Ecod! She can't draw it from any other 'cos they all be empty. There ain't much in the house except a sheriff's officer and nobody's likely to want to eat him – he be too tough.
Robert: In difficulties, Mr. Marks? That's bad news. You must tell us all about it over the ale. I've tobacco for both of us. Here – take a pipe with me now.

> LUKE *takes the pouch and fills his pipe.* PHOEBE *enters with two tankards of ale which she puts on the table.*

Phoebe: Here you are, sir. Drink up now. *(She stays right of table)* You have come straight from the Court, I suppose, sir?
Robert: Not very long ago – this afternoon.
Phoebe: And Sir Michael, poor gentleman – is he better?

Robert: I fear not.
Phoebe: And my lady, sir – was she quite well?
Robert *(aside)*: This is strange. I heard that Phoebe was herself at the Court this very afternoon. Why then should she ask these questions – unless the visit was intended to be a secret? *(Aloud)* Yes, quite well. You knew Lady Audley, did you not, before her marriage when she was –
Phoebe: Miss Graham. Oh, yes, sir. I lived at Mrs. Dawson's when Miss Graham was governess there.
Robert: Indeed. Was she long in the surgeon's family?
Phoebe: Nigh upon two years, sir.
Robert: And she came from London?
Phoebe: Yes, sir.
Robert: And she was an orphan, I believe.
Phoebe: Yes, sir.
Robert: Always as gay and lighthearted as now?
Phoebe: Always, sir.
Robert *(aside)*: This is a woman who can keep a secret. It would take a clever lawyer to bother her in cross examination.
Luke: Enough of this ale. Fetch the bottle girl.
Phoebe: Not tonight, Luke – not tonight for heaven's sake.
Luke *(turning on her)*: Fetch it, I say – do you hear me?

Exit PHOEBE *right.*

Luke *(to* ROBERT*)*: I can't sleep without a nip out of the bottle – it be my nightcap. And what is more I need something to keep the cold out. I've had the 'roomaticks' ever since we came here.
Robert: Yes, it's a poor place. Why, with your interests at Audley Court, you might have done better, surely.
Luke: Better if folks hadn't been so stingy. I might have had a public house at Brentwood or Chelmsford instead of this rotten old place. What's fifty pounds – why if I had –
Phoebe *(re-entering from right with a bottle)*: We forgot the brewhouse door, Luke. Will you come with me and help me put up the bar?
Luke: Give me that bottle, girl *(snatches it and drinks from the bottle)* Brewhouse door can bide for tonight. I ain't moving

again now I've got me hands on this bottle.
Phoebe: I don't feel easy about that brewhouse door, Luke. There are always tramps about.
Luke: Go and put the bar up yourself then, can't you?
Phoebe: It's too heavy for me to lift.
Luke: Then let it bide, if you be too fine a lady to see to it yourself. You be very anxious all of a sudden about this brewhouse door. I suppose you don't want me to open my mouth to this gent – that's about it.
Robert *(quickly changing the subject)*: Then you don't particularly like to live at Mount Stanning?
Luke: No, I don't, and I don't care who knows it. I say again – what's fifty pounds? Come to that, what's a hundred?
Phoebe: Luke! Luke!
Luke: No, no, you'll not stop my mouth again with all your 'Lukes'. I say again – what's a hundred pounds?
Robert *(looking at* PHOEBE *as he speaks to* LUKE*)*: What indeed, Mr. Marks, to a man like you – possessed of the powers you – or rather your wife – holds over the person in question?
Luke *(looking at* PHOEBE*)*: What? You know?
Robert: More than some people give me credit for.
Luke: But you want to know still more, eh, Mr. Counsellor? *(Aside)* He's not such a fool as I thought him to be.
Robert: Knowledge, as the copy book tells us, is power.
Luke: And knowledge may only be had by paying for it and paying handsomely what is more.

Bell rings off left.

Phoebe: The bell! Who can that be at this hour?
Luke: Go and see and you'll find out. If it's another gentleman with a sheriff's card, tell him as we're full and can't accommodate him.

Exit PHOEBE *left.*

Robert *(aside)*: He wants money badly and would sell his soul for a hogshead of cider. But how can I depend upon him? Audley Court is a richer mine to work than Fig Tree Court.

Enter PHOEBE *left. She crosses to* LUKE *and whispers in an agitated manner.*

Luke: What – she here at this time of night? And walked did you say?

Phoebe: The whole way from the Court alone. It's about the rent. She said she could not bear to think of us in trouble.

Robert (*aside*): Lady Audley! Late indeed for an autumn walk. Could an action of charity be the motive for such a rash proceeding? (*Rising – aloud*) Well, goodnight, my worthy host. (*Aside*) I wonder whether there's a lock to my door (*aloud*) Which is my room?

Phoebe: I'll show you at once, sir.

Robert: Don't bother. I can find my way if you direct me.

Phoebe: Very well, sir. It's the room at the top of the stairs on the right.

Robert: Thank you. I'll send up to the Court tomorrow for my traps. Hot water please at half past eight (*moves to down right*) Goodnight again.

Phoebe: Goodnight, sir. (*Exit* ROBERT *down right*).

Phoebe (*to* LUKE): Keep sober for a few minutes, if you can, Luke if you don't wish to ruin us.

Enter LADY AUDLEY *left. Music cue 22 (short).*

Luke: What's your business here?

Lady A: My business, Luke Marks, is to pay your debts – not for your sake but for that of your wretched wife.

Luke: You could have sent the money to Phoebe. You didn't have to come yourself. We don't want no fine ladies up here, pryin' and pokin' their noses into everything.

Phoebe: Luke, Luke! When my lady has been so kind!

Luke: She's been kind, has she? Thank you for nothing. I know the value of her kindness, she'd be uncommon kind, I dessay, if she warn't obligated to be it.

Lady A: Stop! I didn't come here in the dead of night to listen to your insolence. How much is the debt?

Luke: Fourteen pounds odd.

Lady A: Here's fifteen pounds – now go, for I've something to say to your wife.

Luke (*moving up right – aside*) She'll pay for this some day. (*Exit*).

Phoebe: You mustn't go home alone, my lady. You'll let me go with you?

Lady A *(crossing to* PHOEBE*)*: Yes, yes, you shall go home with me. Not a word to Robert Audley that I am here.

Phoebe: Not a word.

Lady A: In which room does he sleep?

Phoebe *(surprised at the question)*: The front room my lady – the one next to ours.

Lady A: The front room?

Phoebe: Yes, my lady. He has gone to bed now.

Lady A: And how long is he to stay here?

Phoebe: He said he was going to stay for a few days, my lady.

Lady A *(aside)*: A few days! Yes, he'll do it – he'll keep his word to his dead friend – unless some strange calamity befalls him and stills his tongue for ever.

Phoebe: I'll give you a receipt for the money, my lady and see Luke safe away. If I wasn't careful to look after him, heaven knows what might happen. We might all be burned in our beds.

Exit up right.

Music cue 23.

Lady A *(moving to centre stage)*: Burned in their beds! He sleeps in the front room. Why this old lath and plaster house would burn like tinder in a moment. Those letters still in his keeping – his threat to expose me – if I was to – Dare I defy him? Dare I? Will he stay his hand now that he has gone so far? Will anything stay it but death? *Music ends.*

Phoebe *(entering up right and coming to* LADY AUDLEY*)*: Here's the receipt my lady. Why, how pale and ill you look.

Lady A: I think I'm going to faint. Where can I get some cold water?

Phoebe: The pump is in the wash house, my lady. *(Pulling out a chair)* You sit down here and I'll run and get you a glass of water.

Lady A: No, no, no, I'll get it myself. I must dip my head in a basin of water if I am to save myself from fainting. Give me a candle. I'll go into your room to get some water for my head.

Phoebe (*picking up one of the two candles on the centre table*): I'll show you the way.

Lady A: No, stay where you are and see that that brute of a husband of yours doesn't follow me.

Phoebe: Very well, my lady. He's in the bar putting up the shutters.

Lady A: Give me the candle then. (*She takes it and exits down right*).

Phoebe (*alone*): Poor soul, she trusts me still. Why did I ever marry Luke? Because I feared him. Often and often I've made up the very sentence I meant to say to him, but I dare not give it utterance. I've watched him many a time sitting on the style trimming a hedge stake with his big clasp knife until I've thought he was just one of those who decoyed their sweethearts into lonely places and murdered them for being false to their word.

Lady A (*re-entering without the candle*): Phoebe!

Phoebe: Yes, my lady?

Lady A (*moving to the exit left*): I'm ready – come.

Phoebe: But the light – you've left it – the light!

Lady A: The wind blew it out as I was leaving your room. I left it there.

Phoebe (*looking towards the stairs down right*): In my room, my lady?

Lady A: Yes, yes, come.

Phoebe: Are you quite sure it was out?

Lady A: I tell you yes. Why do you worry me about your candle? It is past one o'clock. Come Phoebe, come. (*Aside*) 'Tis done – a short while and this house and my enemies too will be ashes. Once more I shall be free, free!

Exit followed by PHOEBE, *Who blows out the candle on the table.*

After a moment a red light is seen off stage right. LUKE *staggers in from up right.*

Luke: Now I *am* drunk – that last strong dose has settled me.

Where's the other light? Can't hardly see? *(Blunders forward and knocks against the chair right)* A man is more drunk in darkness than *(sees red light off)* Why, what's that? *(Staggers to stage right)* The old house is on fire. Phoebe! Phoebe! Help! Help! *Music cue 24 to end of act.* *(Staggers and falls – trying to get up)* Oh, mercy, mercy, save me someone. *(Coughs loudly)* I choke – I choke! – I die! Mercy! Help! Help! *– He falls back as*

THE CURTAIN FALLS
ON
ACT TWO

ACT THREE
SCENE ONE

Music cue 25.

The Lime Tree Walk – later that night. Enter PHOEBE *and* LADY AUDLEY *from left.*

Lady A: Keep close to me. Phoebe. *(Looks off left).*
Phoebe: Why do you look back, my lady?
Lady A: I thought I heard a noise.
Phoebe: It's only the wind in the lime trees, my lady. We are in the Walk. We are almost home.
Lady A: How weary the way has seemed. Every minute seemed like an hour.
Phoebe: The storm has almost ceased.
Lady A *(moving to centre stage – aside)*: But not the storm within my breast. It rages still. *(Aloud – holding out her hand to* PHOEBE*)* Come, child.
Phoebe *(taking* LADY AUDLEY'S *hand)*: How cold your hand is, my lady. It is like marble.
Lady A *(aside)*: As my heart.
Phoebe: I'll see you to your room, my lady and then I'll go back to the inn.
Lady A: But I won't hear of it. You'll stay the night, Phoebe.
Phoebe: Oh, my lady, I dare not. I cannot leave Luke alone.
Lady A: Why not? What harm can come to him? Anyway, is his life so precious?
Phoebe: It isn't that, my lady but –
Lady A: But what, girl?
Phoebe: I must go back.
Lady A: And I say you must not. My mind is made up. Tonight you stay at Audley Court.
Phoebe: Oh, but I must go back, my lady, I forgot –
Lady A: What?

Music cue 26.

Phoebe *(looking off left)*: That Mr. Audley was – Oh, great heavens, my lady – what is that? See there, and there again.
Lady A: Well, child, I see – what of it?

Phoebe: It is a fire – a fire, my lady.

Lady A: Fire? So it is – dear, dear. At Brentwood most likely or further still – quite in the distance. Let me go, Phoebe, it's nothing for us.

Phoebe: Yes, yes, my lady; it's nearer than Brentwood – much nearer. It's in the direction of Mount Stanning.

Lady A: Nonsense, child – it's miles away.

Phoebe: No, no – it's at Mount Stanning. I know it is. It's the Castle Inn that's on fire. I thought of fire tonight and I was fidgety and uneasy, for I knew this would happen some day. I wouldn't mind if it was only the wretched place, but there'll be life lost. There's Luke, too tipsy to help himself, unless others help him. There's Mr. Audley fast asleep and – *(seeing* LADY AUDLEY *smiling triumphantly, struck with a thought, she falls on her knees, clasping her hands)* Oh, my God! Say it's not true, my lady, say it's not true. It's too horrible – it's too horrible – it's too horrible!

Lady A: What's too horrible?

Phoebe: The thought that's in my mind – the dreadful thought that's in my mind.

Lady A *(fiercely)*: What do you mean, girl?

Phoebe: Oh, God forgive me if I'm wrong and God grant I may be! Why did you go up to the Castle, tonight, my lady? You who are so bitter against Mr. Audley and against Luke and who knew they were both under the same roof? Oh, tell me that I do you a cruel wrong, my lady – tell me so – tell me; for as there is a heaven above me, I think that you went to that place tonight on purpose to set fire to it. Tell me that I am wrong, my lady, tell me that I am doing you a wicked wrong!

Lady A *(grasping* PHOEBE's *arm and dragging her to her feet)*: I will tell you nothing except that you are a mad woman. Get up, fool, idiot, coward! Is your husband such a precious bargain that you should be grovelling here, lamenting and groaning for him? What is Robert Audley to you that you behave like a maniac, because you think he is in danger? How do you know that fire is at Mount Stanning? You see a red patch in the sky and you cry out directly that your own paltry

hovel is in flames – as if there was no place in the world that could burn except that. The fire may be at Brentwood, or even farther off. Go then, madwoman, go back and look after your goods and chattels and your husband and your lodger! Go, go, I don't want you.
Phoebe: Oh my lady, forgive me. I don't mind your cruel words. There is nothing you can say to me that is hard enough for having done such a wrong, even in my thoughts, if I am wrong.
Lady A: Go back and see for yourself. I tell you again – I don't want you.

End of music.
PHOEBE *hurries off left.*

It is more than I can bear – suspected – hunted – forced before the world to wreath my face with smiles, and chatter idle gossip, while my heart is torn with torture – is rent with agony. *Music cue 27 to end of scene. (Producing a glass phial from her reticule)* Oh, that I had the courage to swallow but a few drops of this and so end it all for ever. *(Reflecting)* Yet – no – why should I? That girl will never dare to hint her suspicions to the world, and I have nothing now to fear. Luke, in his drunkenness will fall an easy prey, and for the other – I took good care that he should not escape the flames my hands had kindled. Yes, the devouring flame has consumed his life and left nothing of him – nothing but a charred and blackened mass that can tell no tales. *(Moving right)* Yes, Robert Audley – your meddling tongue is silenced for ever – for ever!

She exits laughing hysterically as the

CURTAIN FALLS

ACT THREE
SCENE TWO

The library at Audley Court – the next day. When the curtain rises, LADY AUDLEY *is seated on the sofa on the left end with* SIR MICHAEL *on the right.* ALICIA *is looking out of the window.*

Alicia: No riding today, and no chance of any callers to enliven us – unless that ridiculous Bob comes from Mount Stanning.
Lady A: But he is – *(checks herself suddenly)*.
Alicia: What were you about to say?
Lady A: Nothing – nothing at all. *(Aside)* Little chance of a visit from Mr. Robert Audley today. He has vanished away from the face of this earth, and separated himself for ever from all living creatures.
Sir M: What do you think Major Melville told me when he called here yesterday, Alicia?
Alicia *(moving and sitting in the chair down right)*: I haven't the remotest idea. Perhaps he told you that we should have another war with Russia before long, by Ged, sir!
Sir M: You are an impertinent young miss. Major Melville told me nothing of the kind. He told me that a certain Sir Harry Towers, a very devoted admirer of yours, has forsaken his place in Hertfordshire and his hunting stables for a twelve month's tour.
Alicia: He has gone on the continent has he? Poor fellow – he's a good-hearted stupid creature and twenty times better than that peripatetic, patent refrigerator, Mr. Robert Audley.
Sir M *(gravely)*: I wish, Alicia, you were not so fond of ridiculing Bob. He is a very good fellow, and I'm as fond of him as if he were my own son.
Alicia: But you sent him away from here, yesterday.
Sir M: I am fully aware of that, Alicia. I may be getting old but, as yet I do not think that my brain has begun to atrophy.
Alicia: I am sorry, father. It is just that you spoke so well of him and yesterday you –
Sir M: I hope I shall always be able to speak well of him. I

admit that I have become rather uncomfortable about him lately. He has changed very much within the last few days, and he has taken all sorts of absurd ideas into his head. My lady has alarmed me about him. She thinks –

Lady A: It is better not to say too much about it yet awhile. Alicia knows what I think.

Alicia: Yes, my lady thinks that Bob is going mad; but I know better than that. He's not at all the sort of person to go mad. How should such a sluggish ditch pond of an intellect as his ever work itself into a tempest. He'll never go mad.

Lady A: How slow the time is today – how slow! *(Aside)* Why is there no news of the happenings of last night? Perhaps they were afraid to come and tell him – perhaps they were afraid to break the news to Sir Michael. Who will come and tell it at last, I wonder? The rector of Mount Stanning, perhaps, or the doctor – some important person at least.

Alicia *(who has moved to the window during the last speech)*: The rain seems to have eased off. I think I will go for a turn round the quadrangle. Would you care to join me, Lady Audley?

Lady A: Thank you, no. I have a slight headache. I will remain here for a while and then I think I will go and lie down in my room.

Sir M *(rising)*: I will accompany you, Alicia. The air will do me good.

Alicia: Come then, father.

Exit ALICIA *and* SIR MICHAEL *up left*.

Lady A *(alone)*: Still no news. I think I would rather endure anything than this slow suspense, this corroding anxiety, this insufferable torture. Shall I grow old like this I wonder with every minute of my life seeming like an hour? Shall I never have rest and peace of mind again – never until I am in my grave?

ROBERT *enters from up left and moves to behind the sofa*.

Robert: Lady Audley!

Lady A *(rising)*: Who is that? *(Turning and seeing him)* Robert Audley *(sinks to the ground)*.

Robert *(moving in front of the sofa to right of* LADY AUDLEY*)*:

Lady Audley, I spoke to you yesterday very plainly, but you refused to listen to me.
Lady A *(hiding her face)*: Go away – you are dead! You are dead!
Robert: No, Lady Audley, not dead. And now you must listen to me. There was a fire last night at Mount Stanning, Lady Audley. The Castle Inn, the house in which I slept was burned to the ground. Do you know how I escaped perishing in that destruction?
Lady A *(hoarsely)*: No.
Robert: I escaped by a most providential circumstance. I did not sleep in the room which had been prepared for me. The place seemed wretchedly damp and chilly so I persuaded the servant to make me up a bed upon the sofa in the small ground floor sitting room. Shall I tell you by whose agency the destruction of Castle Inn was brought about, my lady?
Lady A: No, no.

Music cue 29.

Robert: Lady Audley, you were the incendiary! It was you whose murderous hands kindled those flames. It was you who thought that by that thrice horrible deed to rid yourself of me, your enemy and denouncer.

End of music.

Lady A: You lie! You lie!
Robert: Alas no, Lady Audley. It is the truth which I speak, as you know only too well. You wished to rid yourself of me. What did it matter to you that other lives might be sacrificed? You would freely have condemned to death an army of innocent victims. The day is passed for tenderness and mercy. For you I can no longer know pity or compassion. Get up from the floor and listen to what I have to say. *(LADY AUDLEY pulls herself up with the help of the sofa and collapses on to the left end)* Now then – so far as by sparing your shame I can spare others who must suffer by your shame, I will be merciful – but no further – no further, I swear. No life was lost in the fire last night –
Lady A *(looking up)*: None?

Robert: None. It was I who discovered the breaking out of the fire in time to give the alarm and to save the servant girl and that poor drunken wretch Marks – who was burned, in spite of my efforts. *(Crosses to bell cord)*.
Lady A: What are you doing?
Robert: Ringing for one of the servants. *(Pulls the cord)*.
Lady A: Why? What do you want with the servants?
Robert: All in good time, Lady Audley – all in good time. Be patient and you will see. Now then Lady Audley, unless you will confess what you are, and who you are, in the presence of the man you have deceived so long, I will gather together the witnesses who shall swear to your identity and, at the peril of any shame to myself and those I love, I will bring upon you the punishment of your crime.

MARTIN *enters up right. she comes to centre stage.*

Martin: You rang, my lady?
Robert: It was I that rang. Where is your master?
Martin: The master, sir? I believe he is in the garden, sir. Do you want me to take a message to him, sir?
Robert: No – that is all. You may go.
Martin: Very good, sir. *(Exit)*.
Robert: Well, Lady Audley?
Lady A *(rising and dashing the hair from her face)*: All right – you have won! Take me to him – take me to him! *(To centre stage)* I will confess anything – everything! What do I care? Heaven knows I have struggled hard enough against you, and fought the battle patiently enough, but you have conquered, Mr. Robert Audley. It is a great triumph is it not – a wonderful victory? You have used your cool, calculating intellect to a noble purpose. You have conquered a mad woman! *(She begins to laugh)*.

Music cue 30.

Robert *(going to her)*: A mad woman?
Lady A: Yes, when you say that I killed George Talboys, you say the truth.
Robert: Then he is dead!
Lady A: Yes, he is dead. But when you said that I murdered

him foully and treacherously, you lie. I killed him – BECAUSE I AM MAD! Because my intellect is a little way upon the wrong side of that narrow border line between sanity and insanity, because when George Talboys goaded me, as you have goaded me, and reproached me, and threatened me, my mind ,never properly balanced, lost that balance entirely and I was mad – mad – mad!

Music ends.

Robert: This is mere invention to avoid the consequence of your crime.
Lady A: No! I will tell you my secret – the secret which I swore that I would never reveal to a living soul. My mother was mad before me – my mother was sent to a mad house and I have inherited her madness.
Robert: And what of my friend? What of George Talboys?

Music cue 31 to end of scene.

Lady A *(laughing)*: His mangled body lies at the bottom of the old well in Lime Tree Walk. *(To upstage centre – holding out her hands)* Take me to Sir Michael – take me quickly; let him rightly know the woman he has wedded. Let him know she is a bigamist, and incendiary and a murderess! Let him know that she is mad – that she is mad! *(She laughs wildly as*

THE CURTAIN FALLS

ACT THREE
SCENE THREE

The Lime Tree Walk – a few minutes later. SIR MICHAEL AUDLEY *is seated.* ROBERT *enters right followed by* LADY AUDLEY. *He goes to right of the seat.* LADY AUDLEY *remains stage right.*

Robert: Sir Michael, I must speak to you.

Sir M: I was not aware that I had given you permission to return to Audley Court.

Robert: Bear with me, sir, for a few moments. This is a matter of the greatest importance.

Sir M: Very well. What is it? *(Seeing* LADY AUDLEY*)* And why is Lady Audley here?

Robert: She has a confession to make to you, sir – a confession which I know will be a most cruel surprise, a most bitter grief. But it is necessary for your present honour and for your future peace that you should hear it. She has deceived you, I regret to say most basely.

Music cue 32.

Sir M *(rising)*: Deceived me? What is this you are saying? Are you out of your mind?

Robert: It is only right that you should hear from her own lips any excuses which she may have to offer for her wickedness *(breaking down)*: May God soften this blow for you! I cannot.

Sir M *(with a cry of anguish)*: Lucy! Lucy! Tell me that this man is a madman! Tell me so, my love, or I shall kill him!

Music ends.

Lady A *(crossing to* SIR MICHAEL*)*: Would that I could do so, but he has told you the truth and he is not mad. *(Falling on her knees)* I have come to you so that I may confess everything to you. I should be sorry for you if I could, for you have been very, very good to me – much better than ever I deserved; but I can't, I can't. I can feel nothing but my own misery. I laugh at other people's sufferings – they seem so small when I compare them to my own.

Sir M *(taking hold of her and lifting her up)*: Tell me – tell me what it is that you wish to confess. I cannot bear that you should torture yourself so.

Lady A: I will tell you – I will tell you but first I must explain something to you. When I was a very little child, I remember asking where my mother was. They told me she was ill and she was away. One day the secret came out. I worried my foster mother so much to tell me that she flew into a passion and told me that my mother was in a madhouse forty miles away. I brooded upon the thought of my mother's madness. It haunted me day and night until I used to awake in the dead of night screaming aloud in an agony of terror.

Sir M *(taking her in his arms to comfort her)*: My poor child, my poor child. But why should this be judged by my nephew to be a sin? Is this what he is forcing you to confess? If so I will –

Lady A: No – that is not all, alas. I left school before I was seventeen and went to live with my father at Wildersea. There at last, the wandering prince came. His name was George Talboys.

Sir M: George Talboys? *(To* ROBERT*)* Was that not the name of your long lost friend?

Robert: The same.

Lady A: He was the only son of a rich country gentleman. He fell in love with me and married me.

Sir M: Married you?

Lady A: Yes, three months after my seventeenth birthday. I was happy with him as long as his money lasted – for his father had disowned him on our marriage. But when all the money had gone, George grew gloomy and wretched and was always unhappy. Then after my baby was born –

Sir M: A baby? You had a child?

Lady A: Yes – a boy. Dead now, alas, dead. I became irritable and more disposed to complain of poverty and neglect. One day, I upbraided George for his cruelty in having allied a helpless girl to poverty and misery and he flew into a passion with me and left the house. When I awoke the next morning I found a letter telling me he had gone to the Antipodes to seek his fortune and that he would never see me again until he was a rich man. I looked upon this departure as a desertion and the hereditary taint that was in my blood made me subject to fits of violence and despair. I saw my father's eyes fixed on me in horror and alarm and he soothed me as only mad people and children are soothed. Then I determined to desert my father who had more fear of me than love for me. I saw an advertisement in *The Times* and presented myself to the advertiser under a feigned name. The rest you know. I came here and you made me an offer, the acceptance of which lifted me once more into the sphere to which my ambition had pointed ever since I was a schoolgirl.

Sir M: And what of your hus – what of George Talboys?

Lady A: After three years I told myself I had the right to assume him dead and became your wife. Within a month of my marriage, however I read in the papers of the planned return of a certain Mr. Talboys from Australia. I went down to Southampton and told my father everything. We decided that an advertisement of my death should be inserted in *The Times*. Then we discovered that an acquaintance of my father's had a daughter of about my age who was dying. We persuaded the mother to allow him to take this girl over to Ventnor under the name of Mrs. Talboys. There she died and was buried in my name. The advertisement was put in *The Times* and upon the second day after its insertion George Talboys visited Ventnor and saw the grave and the tombstone bearing the name of his wife, Helen Talboys.

Music cue 33.

Sir M *(in a hoarse whisper)*: I cannot hear more. If there is any more to be told, I cannot hear it. *(Crossing to* ROBERT*)* Robert, I shall leave this house tonight – this house in which I have been so happy – perhaps never to return to it. Will you take upon yourself the duty of providing for the safety and comfort of this lady, whom I thought my wife?

Robert: It shall be my solemn duty, sir.

Sir M: I need not ask you to remember in all you do, that I have loved her very dearly and truly. I cannot say farewell to her. I will not say it until I can think of her without bitterness – until I can pity her, as I now pray that God will pity her, this night.

End of music.

(Exit up right).

Robert *(moving to* LADY AUDLEY *who has sunk on to the garden seat during the last speech)*: My uncle may believe you are insane – I do not deem you mad, but dangerous. Yet for all our sakes, madness shall be the supposed excuse for all your crimes, and the rest of your life shall pass in the mad woman's proper home.

Lady A *(rising)*: What mean you?

Robert: A lunatic asylum, my lady!

Lady A *(grasping him)*: No, no, not that, oh heaven, not that!

Robert *(throwing her off)*: It is a fate too merciful for you. Do not forget that you are the murderess of George Talboys.

Lady A *(to stage right)*: But you shall not take me to a madhouse – I will not be buried while yet alive. I am a poor pitiful coward, and have been so from the first – afraid of my mother's inheritance; afraid of poverty, afraid of George Talboys – afraid of you. But you shall not take me to a mad house, you shall not – you shall not.

(Rushes off right).

Robert *(alone)*: I will do that which I think just to others and merciful to her – I will give her time and opportunity for repentance.

Enter ALICIA *right.*

Music cue 34.

Alicia *(to right of* ROBERT*)*: Oh, it's you, Mr. Robert Audley. You will dine with us tonight, I trust. I will –

Robert *(gravely)*: Alicia. Your papa has just endured a great – a very great grief.

Alicia: A grief! Papa grieved? Oh, Robert what has happened?

Robert *(in a low voice)*: I can tell you nothing yet, Alicia.

(Earnestly) Can I trust you?

Alicia: Trust me to do what?

Robert: To be a comfort and a friend to your poor father under a very heavy affliction.

Alicia *(passionately)*: Yes! How can you ask me such a question? Do you think there is anything I would not do to lighten any sorrow of my father's? Do you think there is anything I would not suffer if my suffering could lessen his?

Robert *(quietly)*: No, no. My dear, I never doubted your affection, I only doubted your discretion. May I rely upon that?

Alicia *(resolutely)*: You may, Robert.

Robert: Very well then, my dear girl, I will trust you. Your father is going to leave the Court, for a time at least. The grief which he has just endured has made this place hateful to him. He is going away. But he must not go alone, must he, Alicia?

Alicia: Alone? No, no! But I suppose my lady –

Robert *(moving away left)*: Lady Audley will not go with him. He is about to separate himself from her.

Alicia: For a time?

Robert: No – *(turning to* ALICIA*)* for ever.

Alicia *(moving to* ROBERT*)* Separate himself from her for ever? Then this grief –

Robert: Is connected with Lady Audley. Lady Audley is the cause of your father's sorrow. You will offer to accompany your father wherever he may choose to go, Alicia. Try to be to him what you were before that woman came between you and your father's love.

Alicia: I will, I will!

Robert *(taking* ALICIA *into his arms and kissing her forehead)* My dear Alicia, do this and you will make me very happy. I have been in some measure the means of bringing this sorrow upon your father. Try to restore my uncle's happiness, Alicia and I will love you more dearly than brother ever loved noble hearted sister.

Alicia: But I do not want you to love me as a brother.

Robert: Do you mean – could you mean – that you love me?

Music cue 35.

Alicia: Yes, Robert I love you. I have always loved you – and never as a sister.

Robert: And I love you, Alicia. I love you with all my heart.

Alicia: Robert.

Robert: Alicia – some day – when you return – will you do me the honour of becoming my wife?

Alicia: Yes, Robert, I will. You are a good fellow Bob and I will look after my father as I have promised and see that he learns to forget his troubles. I will go and get ready directly. I shall see you again before we travel?

Music ends.

Robert: Yes, dear. *(He kisses her on the forehead)*.

Exit ALICIA *up right.*

Music cue 36.

Robert *(alone–walking to the well)*: I have kept my promise, George. I have kept my promise. Lie at peace there in your unknown grave for Sir Michael must never know that the woman he has loved bears the brand of murder on her soul. *(Moves to centre stage)*.

Music ends.

Enter SIR MICHAEL *up right.*

Sir M *(moving to right of* ROBERT*)* Farewell.

Robert: You go to London by the mail?

Sir M: Yes.

Robert: Have you any idea of where you will stay?

Sir M: Yes. I shall stop at the Clarendon. I am known there.

Robert: Alicia will accompany you.

Sir M: Alicia?

Robert: She could not very well stay here, you know. It would be best for her to leave the Court until –

Sir M: Yes, yes, I understand. But is there nowhere else she can go? Must she be with me?

Robert: She would not be happy anywhere else.

Sir M *(in a strange subdued voice)*: Let her come then – let her

come. Have you told her about – ?
Robert: I have told her nothing, except that you are about to leave the Court for some time and that you have suffered a great sorrow.
Sir M *(in a broken voice)*: You are very good, my boy – you are very good.
Robert: Oh, sir, how can I ever forgive myself for having brought this grief upon you?
Sir M: No, no, Robert, you did right. I wish that God had been so merciful to me as to take my miserable life before this night – but you did right *(moving to exit up right and turning to face* ROBERT*).* You did right. *(Exit).*

Enter PHOEBE *left supporting* LUKE *who is bandaged.*

Robert: Luke, what are you doing here. You should be in bed. Here, sit down on this bench. *(Helps* LUKE *to bench where he sits with* PHOEBE *beside him.* ROBERT *stands on the right of bench).*
Luke *(as he sits)*: I had to come, Mr. Robert. I had to thank you for saving me from the fire last night.
Robert: I need no thanks, Luke Marks. I was very glad to be of service to you.
Luke: You was uncommon fond of that gent as disappeared, warn't you, sir?
Robert: Yes, yes. He was my very dear friend.
Luke: I heard the servants at the Court say how you took on when you couldn't find him.
Robert: Pray do not speak any more of this subject. I cannot tell you how much it distresses me. *(Moving away right).* *(Turning to face* LUKE*)* You were paid for keeping silent. You had better keep silent still.
Luke: Had I? But suppose my Phoebe had one secret and I another – what then?
Robert: What do you mean?
Luke: Suppose I could have told something all along, and would have told it, perhaps, if I had been a little better treated? How then?
Robert *(moving to right of* MARK*)* I think you had better tell me now.

Luke: Well – it would be the seventh of September last. I was crossing the meadows and the church clock was striking nine. I had been hay making and was in a hurry to get home so I took the short cut through this here Lime Tree Walk. I was close agen the mouth of that well over there when I heard a sound that made my blood creep. It were a groan – a groan of a man in pain lying somewhere hid in the bushes. I began to search and I found a man lying under a lot of laurels. He caught me by the wrist and said 'I want to get away from this place, without being seen by a livin' creature' – that's what he said.

Robert: George – it was George and he's alive! Where is he? What did you do with him?

Luke: I took him to my mother's cottage as that was the nearest place. He was in a bad way. I wanted to fetch Mr. Dawson, but he wouldn't let me. He asked for a piece of paper and he wrote a letter to you which he said I was to give to you after he had gone and then I helped him to the railway station and he went off and I ain't never seen him since that day.

Robert: And the letter? What of the letter?

Luke: Heaven forgive me, sir – I kept it, sir – thinkin' as how I might make a tidy sum out of the matter. I was going to give it to you I swear but when Phoebe here told me how she had seen the gentleman talking to Lady Audley in the Lime Tree Walk that night, well – I put two and two together and I guessed what had happened to him and –

Robert: Yes – I can imagine the rest.

Luke: My Phoebe knew nothing of this, sir – I swear. I told her nought of what happened that night. So I kept the letter and kept my secret.

Robert (*moving away right*): And my lady kept hers. And George, my dear friend George. I wonder where he is now.

George (*entering up right*): Here I am, Robert, my old friend!

Robert (*running to meet him centre stage*): Great heavens –

George – here!
George: Yes, my dear, dear, friend *(they embrace)*.
Robert: I have mourned you as dead and now here you are – alive and well. I have just heard the story from the lips of this man. But how did you escape from the well?
George: I fell upon my feet upon a mass of slush and mire but my shoulder and arm were injured and I was stunned and dazed. But after a while I recovered sufficiently to climb up the side of the well. The stones were rough and uneven and my Australian experiences aided me in my peril. After I had clambered out I lay in the laurel bushes until after dark when this man found me.
Robert: And where have you been? I have searched the country far and wide.
George: I have been to foreign climes to try to forget. But I yearned for the strong clasp of your hand, Bob – the friendly touch of the hand which has guided me through the darkest passage of my life. So I returned to this country. But when I discovered that there had been no letter from you, in return for that which I sent you, I decided to come here to find you and to solve the mystery of –

Enter LADY AUDLEY *up right.* PHOEBE *rises and moves away left.*
Helen!
Robert: She has confessed her crime to Sir Michael and now –

Music cue 38.

Lady A *(breaking down right)*: I shall not go to a madhouse. I shall not – I *(sees* GEORGE*)* Ah, you have returned from the dead to haunt me *(backing to centre stage)* It is his spirit – I have seen it in my dreams – Oh, mercy! Mercy!

Music ends.

George *(moving to her right)*: Helen let it comfort you to know that you have failed in your dreadful purpose. I forgive you of your dreadful wrong. I forgive you.
Lady A: Talk not to me thus. It is to mock my agony, for I am dying!
Robert *(moving to right of* GEORGE*)*: Dying?

Music cue 39.

Lady A *(to* ROBERT*)*: Yes. Your threat – the madhouse. I have taken poison – death is on me even now *(sinking to the ground)*. If I had delayed but a few minutes only! But this torture heaven has reserved for the supreme moment.

Music ends.

Enter ALICIA *and* SIR MICHAEL.

Sir M *(to up centre)*: What is this? What is happening?
Alicia *(running to* ROBERT*)*: Robert, what is it?
Robert: Hush!
Lady A: Do not touch me – do not come near me – 'tis almost over. You will not give my memory to infamy? No – you will not dare. For your own sakes you will not dare and so – buried in the grave with her for ever will be – Lady Audley's secret – ah!

Half raises herself, presses both hands to her heart and falls back dead. TALBOYS *kneels beside her covering his face with his hands.* ROBERT *raises his hand towards heaven as*

THE FINAL CURTAIN FALLS

PRODUCTION NOTES

SETTINGS

This version of the play has been designed so that alternate scenes can be played in front of a drop cloth or traverse curtains thus reducing the time taken to effect a scene change. As the settings are very simple and all the exits either from left or right, back drops could be used for all the settings. An alternative method (used in the production illustrated in this book) is to have the Lime Tree Walk as the main setting and to slide the other settings in front of this by means of boat trucks or the old Victorian method of flats in grooves. The flats need not be more than screen height as the Lime Tree Walk set can act as an exterior backing for the other sets with added effect. The moves given in this acting edition are for the former method.

MUSIC

This play does not include any songs but background music is very important if the authentic atmosphere is to be acheived. Throughout the script cues are given as a guide to the most significant spots for music. A piano score of music written for this play by Brian Daubney is available. Application should be made to ~~G. Combridge Ltd~~. Hanburys Plays

FURNITURE AND PROPERTIES

A full list of the furniture and props referred to in the script is included in this book. Producers may wish to add items of stage dressing to these but, if set changes are to be done swiftly, furniture and properties are best kept to a minimum in this type of play.

LIGHTING

A complete lighting plot is included in this script. It helps, for this type of play if footlights are used – if possible with the old-fashioned shell cowl.

COSTUME

The period of the play is mid-nineteenth century but there is no reason why it should not be presented in any period from then until the turn of the century, providing that the dates mentioned in the script are suitably adjusted.

STYLE OF PERFORMANCE

Although the Victorian versions of this play were intended to be taken quite seriously that would be very difficult – if indeed desirable – today. It should be acted very earnestly in the 'grand manner' with plenty of attack and projection with just an edge of overplaying. The asides must be tackled boldly. Played in this manner it will earn far more laughter than burlesque (as the exponents of the art of playing farce will agree). Unlike the older and cruder melodramas such as 'Sweeney Todd' and Maria Marten' it is doubtful if this play will evoke much audience participation other than laughter and the occasional hiss, boo and cheer.

LIGHTING PLOT

ACT ONE

Scene One — Interior
TO OPEN: A summer morning
NO CUES

Scene Two — Exterior (cloth)
TO OPEN: Late summer, early afternoon, sunny
NO CUES

Scene Three — Interior. Apparent light source is the window up-stage. There is a practical oil lamp on the desk
TO OPEN: Late afternoon, approaching dusk towards end of scene
CUE ONE: ROBERT moves oil lamp to picture – fade light on desk and increase light at easel

Scene Four — Exterior – as Act One Scene Two
NO CUES

ACT TWO

Scene One — Interior – As Act One Scene Three
TO OPEN: Morning
NO CUES

Scene Two — Exterior – As Act One Scene Two
TO OPEN: Morning
NO CUES

Scene Three — Interior. There are two practical candles on the table up centre
TO OPEN: Night – apparent light source – the candles on table
CUE TWO: LADY AUDLEY exits with candle – check half lighting
CUE THREE: PHOEBE BLOWS OUT CANDLE – check all lighting
CUE FOUR: AFTER LADY AUDLEY AND PHOEBE EXIT – an increasing glow of fire from stage right

ACT THREE

Scene One — Exterior as Act One Scene Two
TO OPEN: Night. From the beginning of the scene the glow of a distant fire may be just noticeable from off stage left

Scene Two — Interior – As Act One Scene Three
TO OPEN: A wet dull morning outside. The stage brightens shortly after the beginning of the scene as the rain stops

Scene Three — Exterior – As Act One Scene Two
TO OPEN: A dull morning after rain
NO CUES

PROPERTY PLOT

ACT ONE

Scene One	The Times – ROBERT
	Letter – ROBERT
	Beer and two glasses set on DESK
Scene Two	Wood for whittling – LUKE
	Knife – LUKE
	Reticule containing handkerchief
	card case
	package with baby shoe
	yellow hair Set R. of WELL
Scene Three	Sketching materials – LADY AUDLEY
	Package of shoe and hair – PHOEBE
	Reticule set on SOFA
	Easel containing picture covered with green baize
	Oil lamp set on DESK
Scene Four	Handkerchief – LADY AUDLEY

ACT TWO

Scene One	The Times – ROBERT
	Papers set on DESK
	Box of cigars and matches set on DESK
Scene Two	Novel – ALICIA
Scene Three	Two candles (*lit*) in bottles set on TABLE
	Tankard – LUKE
	Pouch of tobacco and pipe – ROBERT
	Pipe – LUKE
	Two tankards – PHOEBE, set off R.
	Bottle – PHOEBE, set off R.
	Reticule containing money – LADY AUDLEY
	Receipt – PHOEBE, set off R.

ACT THREE

Scene One	Reticule containing phial of poison – LADY AUDLEY
Scene Two	——
Scene Three	——

FURNITURE PLOT

ACT ONE

Scene One TABLE L.C.
CHAIR U.S. of TABLE
CHAIR L. of TABLE
SOFA R.C.

Scene Two GARDEN SEAT L.C.
WELL R.

Scene Three SOFA L.
DESK U.R.C.
CHAIR behind DESK

Scene Four As Act One Scene Two

ACT TWO

Scene One As Act One Scene Three
Scene Two As Act One Scene Two
Scene Three WOODEN TABLE C.
WOODEN SETTLE U.S. of TABLE
CHAIR L. of TABLE
CHAIR R. of TABLE

ACT THREE

Scene One As Act One Scene Two
Scene Two As Act One Scene Three
Scene Three As Act One Scene Two